CONQUER

THE

FAT-LOSS

CODE

WENDY CHANT, MPT, SPN

New York Chicago San Francisco Lisbon London Madrid Mexico City
Milan New Delhi San Juan Seoul Singapore Sydney Toronto

Library of Congress Cataloging-in-Publication Data

Chant, Wendy.
    Conquer the fat-loss code / by Wendy Chant.
        p.   cm.
    Includes index.
    ISBN-13: 978-0-07-163007-8 (alk. paper)
    ISBN-10: 0-07-163007-4 (alk. paper)
    1. Weight loss.   2. Energy metabolism.   3. Biological rhythms.   I. Title.

    RM222.2.C4393   2009
    613.2'5—dc22   2009004671

1 2 3 4 5 6 7 8 9 10 11 12 13 14 15 16 17 18 19 20 21 22 23 24   FGR/FGR   0 9

ISBN   978-0-07-163007-8
MHID   0-07-163007-4

Illustrations by Visual Health Information

McGraw-Hill books are available at special quantity discounts to use as premiums and sales promotions or for use in corporate training programs. To contact a representative, please visit the Contact Us pages at www.mhprofessional.com.

All information written in this guide or presented orally is the property of ForeverFit Lifestyle Centers, Inc., and such information may not be reproduced in any form without written consent from ForeverFit Lifestyle Centers, Inc.

ForeverFit Lifestyle Centers, Inc., and its staff do not represent themselves as medical or nutrition professionals. ForeverFit Lifestyle Centers, Inc., its staff, and programs make no claim to recommend, diagnose, treat, or cure any disease or complication by any holder or purchaser of this material. It is under the strong advice of ForeverFit Lifestyle Centers, Inc., that any and all individuals seek advice from their health care professional before undertaking any exercise or nutrition plan.

ForeverFit® is a registered identity of ForeverFit Lifestyle Centers, Inc. Nutrition Boot Camp™ is a trademark of ForeverFit Lifestyle Centers, Inc., and no entity may use or market Nutrition Boot Camp.

This book is printed on acid-free paper.

Thanks, Lord Jesus, for the healing power and strength you give me every day.

To my daughter, Valerie, truth and faith bring peace and joy. Keep your integrity and faith, and the Lord will give you love and every joy life has to offer. Mommy loves you!

Contents

Foreword

The art of healing comes from nature, not from the
physician. Therefore the physician must start from
nature, with an open mind.

—*Philipus Aureolus Paracelsus*

At the Center for Natural and Integrative Medicine, we believe
the best approach to your health is an integrative one, giving
you the benefits of both natural and conventional medicine to
restore optimal health and balance.

Wendy Chant and I share this philosophy with our clients
and patients, respectively, and have been sending referrals to
one another for years. When I have a patient who expresses a
need for more movement or dietary discretion in his or her life,
my first thought—and recommendation—is Wendy. When she
has clients whose needs go beyond mere physical and dietary
changes, she sends them to me, so I can restore their hormonal
balance. This way, her clients and my patients can achieve maximum balance for cellular health.

Life is all about equilibrium; at least, that's the view that
Wendy and I share. Wendy's philosophy is based on balanc-
ing what you eat and how you move. In *Crack the Fat-Loss
Code*, she introduced the idea that creating a sense of balance
in the body was essential to restoring the proper levels of fat
and muscle. In this new book, she focuses on how what you eat
and when you move create a new sense of balance designed to
readjust your metabolism for life.

Conquer the Fat-Loss Code speaks to more than just weight
loss or physical fitness; it speaks to the daily balance that must
exist within the body's cells to provide maximum health ben-

efits. This book accomplishes what Wendy and I both try to do in our private practices: build a bridge toward wellness.

Many people might see this as just another diet book, but to do so would be to miss out on most of its benefits. In this volume, Wendy shares groundbreaking information about how your body needs, digests, and uses the food you eat. The body is full of complex pathways, delivery routes, organs, and systems that defy description. Wendy shares both essential information and the routines to help you understand how important it is to incorporate physical fitness with nutrition for fat loss.

Her program goes beyond weight loss or muscle building; everything she writes about is carefully designed to promote function and balance within each of the body's millions of cells. When cellular balance is achieved, you have more control over your body—whether to lose weight; get in shape; or simply balance all the areas of your body, mind, and soul.

We are all born with genetic factors that influence our lives. Many people feel they are doomed—or at least defined—by these factors, but it is my philosophy that genes affect only 20 percent of how we live; the other 80 percent is determined by the daily choices we make when it comes to things like nutrition, fitness, lifestyle, and more.

We all want beautiful, radiant skin; a smaller waist; and optimal health, but if we don't have the proper diet and exercise program, these results can't exist. *Conquer the Fat-Loss Code* covers both eating and movement to create balance in your body so that you can achieve your personal nutrition and fitness goals. I recommend it highly, both as a physician and as a friend!

—Kirti M. Kalidas, M.D., N.D.
The Center for Natural and Integrative Medicine
drkalidas.com

Acknowledgments

This was an incredibly important book for me. The time in which it was completed was a sheer miracle, and it certainly wouldn't have had a chance without the incredible work of my writing authority, Rusty Fischer. Thank you, Rusty, once again for your true professionalism and incredible writing ability; you're an amazing talent and a gifted writer.

Thanks to my literary agent, Wendy Sherman, who continues to believe in me and my message and mission to help the world become fit.

Special thanks to the team at McGraw-Hill: my editors, Judith McCarthy, Fiona Sarne, and Nancy Hall for their hard work in publishing this book on such a tight deadline. I appreciate the continued opportunity they have given me to spread my message.

Thanks to the love of my life, Scott, who has been my true friend and soul mate. Thanks for your love and support, babe. I love you.

Special appreciation and eternal gratitude to my dear friend Diane Breen, who has always been there through good and bad times to advise me, lend a hand, and be a true friend. I love you, my friend.

Many thanks to Debbie Cumming and Cathy Marques for helping with some parts of this book.

Special appreciation goes to this wonderful group of divinely sent true friends who have seen me through so much this past year. I will always hold their love, support, and prayers dear. Thanks in friendship to Ann and Tom Holstein, Jannet Abraham-Clark, Ray Clark, Susan Johnson, Jerrie Griffee, Darlean Yankovich, Sonja and Chris Smith, Laura Tappen Brown, Sandy Ambrose, Jana Weiner, Ina Williams, Debbie Barnes,

Cindy Bradley, MC Teet, Denise Charlesworth, Vicky McVay, Fenton Froom, Donielle Deitz, Blanch Torres, Jan Newell, Christine and Jim Carlton, Janne Ackerman, Connie Jones, Monica Wofford, Melissa and Frank Grisson, Karen Rhine, and Debbie and Jim Guthrie for their continued support.

Love to my brother Tom and nephew Robbie.

Special gratitude to Dr. Matthew Albert and Dr. Robert Reynolds and the staff of the Cancer Institute of Florida for the kindness and hope they have given me and the special work they do for all cancer warriors.

Introduction

Get Ready to Take Fat Loss
to a Whole New Level

I love this book and eating plan! I have been on the
plan for four weeks, have seen a significant change
in my body, and have reduced my fat content. The
program is easy to follow and makes total sense.
It does not restrict too much and allows you to
eat normal food. It does not require eating yogurt,
cucumbers, and peanut butter, which most diet
plans insist on. The recipes included in the book are
great. This is a lifetime eating plan, not a diet! With
exercise, I am having great results.

—*C. Warren, proud code cracker*

Congratulations, fellow code crackers! Today we come together
to celebrate the next new adventure in fat loss. My guess is
that you've enjoyed some measure of success from reading my
first book, *Crack the Fat-Loss Code*, and now you're ready for
more.

Maybe you've lost ten or twenty pounds and a few inches
from your waistline. Maybe you started the program, fell off the
wagon, started back up again, and are now starting to get the
rhythm of cracking the code. Or maybe you're new to the whole
code-cracking concept, have never heard of me before, and don't
really know what I'm talking about yet; in this case, I welcome

you warmly to the fold. (Don't worry; you'll catch on quickly.) Whatever stage you're at, we have a lot to cover, so I want to get straight to it.

I'm Baaack!

This book is called *Conquer the Fat-Loss Code*, and the key word here is *conquer*. We all want to conquer our diets, don't we? I mean, nobody buys a diet book to *gain* weight. But sometimes we need a little help after we've been on a program for longer than two weeks.

If I were there with you every day, urging you along, patting you on the back, whispering advice in your ear, putting fresh broccoli in your shopping cart, and lacing up your jogging shoes, maybe there wouldn't be a need for this book. But I'm not, so this will be your personal trainer, planner, and motivator.

Think of this book as me knocking on your door to remind you how great that peanut butter smoothie tastes or to urge you to add a few pounds to those bicep curl bars you bought last month. It can be difficult to succeed when you get too comfortable with your routine. That's why I was eager to write this book quickly, within a year of publishing *Crack the Fat-Loss Code*. I know how frustrating it can be when you don't have support a week, a month, three months, a year, or even two years into a new lifestyle plan; support and extra motivation are key.

That's why you're here today. In an effort to face the future head-on, this book gives you a way to keep losing fat, learn new ways to reprogram your metabolism, and track your success.

It's Time to Quit "Recycle Dieting"

I like to think of the program in my books not as a diet but as a lifestyle. That's probably a new concept for a lot of you. With most diets, you don't care when things get stale—you lose some weight and enjoy yourself, but then the weight comes right back as soon as you're done with the Peanut Butter and Jelly Diet or the Cantaloupe and Cottage Cheese Plan. So you move on to the next new thing, say the Coffee and Croissant Program.

I call this "recycle dieting." You never stick with one plan because, frankly, most of them are flawed, and you simply recycle the old diet plan for a new one and begin all over again. But since you're so used to throwing one thing away after a few months and starting something else, maybe you're feeling a little stuck right now and thinking, "What next?"

Like anything lasting and worthwhile—a marriage, a home, a career—a lifestyle can be hard to maintain, especially in our busy times. After all, we're taught to want it all, want it now, and get it even sooner, but most of us live in the short term. We rush through the day and crash into bed at night, not having the time, focus, or energy to concentrate on what we ate or how we moved.

Lifestyles are tricky. They call for the long-term, goal-setting, careful-planning type of energy and enthusiasm that can sometimes be hard to maintain once those first few pounds come off and you've bragged about it to all your friends.

Think about most of the diets you've been on. You start out all excited, get some quick results by eating nothing but cheese or yogurt or peanut butter or bacon for a few days, and then after a while you lose your enthusiasm but no more weight. In fact, once the enthusiasm wears off, the weight typically comes back.

My program is different. It was designed to stand the test of time; to be flexible; and to include cheat days, carbohydrate-rich ("carb-up") days, and days when food is the last thing on your mind. Best of all, it was specifically designed to address the dreaded dieter's plateau.

Crack the Fat-Loss Code introduced the main concepts you need to be more focused about including movement and good nutrition in your life. The best part is you can do it in a way that's natural for you: you pick what to eat on your cheat days; you decide what carbs to splurge on when you can; and you decide how you move, for how long, and how often.

Conquer the Fat-Loss Code kicks things up a notch. This means accelerating your program just a tad to lose even more fat with advanced meal plans. It combines the right foods with the right exercises at the right time. And most important, it makes it easier for you to track your success.

The pages of this new book are filled with what I've been teaching my advanced classes for years. Now I'm sharing these secrets with you to help you "conquer the code" and truly live fit forever.

Conquering the Fat-Loss Code

I'm really excited about this book! *Conquer the Fat-Loss Code* is the best guide to achieving long-term success in getting and staying healthy. Like a mother who loves all her children equally, I'm proud of both of my books, but this second one is a little easier to follow than the first, with a format that allows you to track your progress regularly. Specifically, it gives you daily target plans that tell you exactly what to eat and when to eat, using either your own recipes or any of the many suggestions in the expanded recipe section.

The target plans also provide ideas for the best fat-burning exercises and, most important, the best time to exercise to optimize fat loss. Properly timing your exercise can increase your weight loss by as much as 80 percent. Target planning makes success easy to achieve and ensures day-to-day accountability while you record your progress with your personal success tracker.

What, exactly, will you get in *Conquer the Fat-Loss Code?* I'm glad you asked. First we'll start with Part 1, in which I'll give you a brief overview on understanding the code, the secrets to macro-patterning meal plans, and exercise tips that will optimize fat loss. You will be able to minimize the amount of exercise you do but maximize your results. By combining my meal plans and the timing of exercise, you'll melt fat even faster.

Next, in Part 2, I'll give you all the tools you'll need to conquer the fat-loss code for the rest for your life. This section includes secrets to using advance meal planning to continue to outsmart your body and increase your metabolism, tips for continuing to drop weight faster, and eight more weeks of sample meal plans to outsmart your metabolism. We also give you the secrets to exercise timing to maximize your results and minimize your exercise time. Best of all, I'll give you one of the greatest tools I've ever come across in the battle against fat. The revolutionary daily success planners provide daily meal plans, a place to record your fat-loss progress, and a source of inspiration and support for the road ahead. For every day of the meal plan cycles, you will know what to eat, how much, and when, plus what you can substitute, what supplements you should take, and what kind of exercise you should do to maximize your weight loss.

Part 3 will address things like flexible meal planning to accommodate weekends, traveling, holidays, and time off. Since conquering the code is a lifestyle plan, I offer you dozens of ways to stay on target during those tempting holiday feasts, vacations, and times when you need to restructure your meal plan a bit. Another important topic covered in this section is what to do if you fall off the wagon. It's easy to slip, but that doesn't mean you should give up. If you do find yourself cheating during this eight-week program, I have several ways for you to jump-start, revitalize, or even start over so that you're back on track before you ever realize you were off.

Part 4 gives you more of the recipes you need to conquer the code, and I've labeled each recipe to indicate with which meal plan it works best. For instance, I've classified recipes as good for carb-up days, carb-down days, or baseline days. You'll know right away which recipe goes with which meal plan day.

Are you ready to conquer the fat-loss code and start shedding those pounds? Let's get started, code crackers!

What the Code Crackers Are Saying

Cindy Bradley

*The day I was intro-
duced to Wendy
Chant and ForeverFit
changed my life forever.
I had been battling
my weight since my
early thirties. I lost
my mother in 1988,
went through a painful
divorce in 1991,
and lost my father
in 1998. For twenty
years, I handled all my
emotional stress with food.*

*My doctors warned me that my weight would
become a factor in the future if I did not take
control of my life. One even told me I would never
be able to lose the weight without gastric bypass
surgery. I was mortified and angry about his
comments and decided to prove him wrong.*

*I called my friend Cathy, who had told me
about Wendy and ForeverFit a year before. Cathy
made an appointment for me to meet with Wendy,
and my life changed that day.*

*My first meeting with Wendy was humbling
at best, and she gave me the three things I needed
most: support, courage, and hope. Once I started
the program, I realized it was doable because I can
eat any food I want—it's just limited to certain
days. I travel a tremendous amount for my job,
and I've found that I can be successful even away*

from home. All restaurants will accommodate me if I just ask. I lost all of my excuses once I was on the plan. If I can do it, so can you. I know that sounds simple, and it really is.

Today I have lost eighty pounds and almost as many inches! For the first time in many years, I have the hope of being successful and the vision of my new, healthy lifestyle.

Wendy gave me hope; I have taken control of my life and will be forever grateful to her. My

life has always been amazing, even with all the losses, but I now have an even more amazing present and future—and you can too. I am not where I want to be yet, but I am well on my way, and I absolutely know I will make it and be forever fit.

PART 1

Conquering the Code

1

Understanding the Code and the Secrets to Fat Loss

What does it really mean to conquer the fat-loss code? You're about to find out. Here are the real "meat and potatoes" of how you're going to reprogram your metabolism to melt fat and lose weight—forever. A big part of the program is to understand the body's seventy-two-hour/forty-eight-hour response pattern to eating. Yes, there *is* a specific pattern to how your body responds to what you eat, and 72/48 is the code for losing fat.

How do you beat this code? The 72 refers to your body's response to food intake. Every seventy-two hours, your body analyzes the energy you take in and calculates how it can reserve as much of that energy as possible to allow it to function as it should. The 48 refers to your body's response to energy expenditure. Every forty-eight hours, your body slows certain functions, or readjusts the amount of energy it uses, so that it has enough in reserve to keep functioning based on what it thinks you'll expend. To survive, your body has to keep the amount of energy it takes in and the amount of energy it expends in balance. The secret to conquering fat loss is to manipulate where your body gets its energy, and we're going to trick it into using fat as its energy source.

Macro-Patterning to Manipulate Energy Stores

Now that you know the secret to the fat-loss code, you should also understand another concept called *macro-patterning*. This is the process of manipulating energy stores so your body can use all its excess fat, as well as the food you eat, much more efficiently as immediate energy and not store fat.

Macro-patterning means carefully regulating and alternating protein, fat, and carbohydrate intake to combat your body's adaptive response to your eating patterns; this allows you to manipulate something called glycogen. *Glycogen* is just a fancy word for the stored energy that comes from carbohydrate consumption. Your body automatically chooses carbohydrates rather than fat as its main source of energy because carbohydrates are instantly available.

Remember, your body is a machine with many operating functions, and if food is its fuel, what happens when you're not eating? Where does it go to get fuel, and what does it use once it gets there? Your body is still functioning even when you're not putting food in your mouth, and the next source of fuel it taps into is the glycogen stored in your body's muscles and liver. Only when glycogen stores are low—from reducing carbohydrates or creating an energy deficit through exercise—will your body find and use excess fat for fuel. Understanding the 72/48 code lets us manipulate and reduce glycogen stores in the body and use excess fat.

Remember, the minute your body thinks you're on a diet, it will do anything and everything it can to hold on to as much fat as possible because it knows you're going into starvation mode. Your brain will send the rest of your body a signal to conserve energy for the coming dry spell. That means it shuts down body temperature, reduces the absorption rate of food, and slows down your metabolism, all with the intention of storing more fat so it will have plenty of energy "just in case."

By focusing on good nutrition and macro-patterning, you can trick your body into using fat as an energy source and feel great while doing it! With my new meal plans, you also take fat loss to a more advanced level, forcing your body to "melt" fat more efficiently and stop its automatic conservation of fat.

Macro-Patterning and Food Plan Cycles

By macro-patterning using food plan cycles, you will lower glycogen levels a few days a week just enough for your body to use fat as a source of energy, and then you will replace those stores so your body doesn't think you're starving yourself. If your body perceives starvation, it will store fat. It's kind of like sleight of hand; from time to time you have to trick your body into thinking it's not losing fat when it actually is. These cycles continually repeat themselves during an eight-week period (see Part 2 for your personalized eight-week cycle).

So how do you trick your body? By alternating your meal plans on various days to change your carb, fat, and protein intake and stop your body's adaptive response. As you will see when I lay out the meal plans for you, each cycle consists of certain "cycle days" that tell you how to eat on that specific day. For example, there is carb-up day (D), carb-down day (C), baseline day (B), grapefruit day (GF), zero starch day (ZS), cheat day (CH), and so on. We'll get into more detail about the different days when I give you an overview of specific meal plans.

Some of you may be beginners at code cracking, and others may have already completed the eight-week program in *Crack the Fat-Loss Code*. Either way, understanding the code is the first step to conquering it. So whether you're a newbie or a veteran, you'll find that my program and advance meal planning will help you begin, continue, and maintain your fat-loss journey.

> ### Conquer the Code
> Macro-patterning shifts the food in your typical everyday diet to different days. Just as later in the book I suggest that you "switch up" your exercise routines from day to day and week to week, eating in this same way will continually trick your body into using fat rather than storing it.

Using Supplements for Optimal Fat Loss

Now that you understand how to conquer the code, I'll show you how to maximize fat loss by combining supplements with macro-patterning. Few people consider the role vitamins, minerals, and other supplements play in taking off fat. However, the human body has specific controls to regulate such factors as metabolism, muscle mass, and body fat, so the more often your body runs at peak performance through supplement use, the more effective it will be at maintaining these factors at appropriate levels.

Often when people reach for a pill or capsule to regulate their weight, they are looking for a quick fix or swallowing the latest weight-loss fad. But supplementation is the act of restoring your body's natural balance so it can do what it needs to do naturally. Three supplements are especially helpful in helping control your body's fat stores: L-carnitine, lipotropics, and green tea.

L-Carnitine

L-carnitine is known as a fat-loss transporter. The primary function of the amino acid carnitine is to facilitate the transport of fatty acids from a cell's cytoplasm across the mitochondrial membrane to the interior of the mitochondria, where fat burning takes place. Without carnitine as a carrier, the fatty acids remain in the cytoplasm (think of it as in storage), and you won't lose as much fat. L-carnitine (from natural and/or synthetic sources) is taken as a supplement because our bodies are unable to get it in enough of the quantities needed from food we take in, thanks to changes such as the decline of grass-fed cattle and other impurities in our food supply. Take L-carnitine prior to and immediately after exercise, especially when you exercise in the morning. It is best in liquid form (read the label instructions for the correct dosage).

Lipotropics

Lipotropics or fat emulsifiers are scientifically engineered to assist in the breakdown, distribution, and burning (oxidation) of fatty acids. The active ingredients actually accelerate the fat-burning process by breaking down fat cells into smaller particles (emulsification) to be used as fuel during exercise.

Take lipotropics prior to and immediately after exercise, especially when you exercise in the morning. It is best in liquid form because quick absorption is key to its effectiveness. (Read the label instructions for the correct dosage.)

Green Tea

Metabolic enhancers provide the body with a "spark" that aids in the production of heat once fat is transported and has been emulsified. This is like the fireplace in your house—the place where fat is taken to be burned and produce heat. This is where we also get the term *fat burning*. Green tea is a great metabolic enhancer. In extract form, it has been shown to heat up your body's core temperature by 4 percent, which can mean a loss of six to eight pounds monthly without a change of diet. Beware of soft drinks that are "green tea flavored," as these aren't potent enough to promote fat loss. Instead, look for an extract that is concentrated specifically for fat loss.

Look for extracts you dilute in water and drink as you would a soda; green tea may be taken once or twice daily. Since you are helping your body increase its core temperature, I suggest that you cycle on and off this product. For example, note when you start using the product, take it until the package is used up, and then stay off of it for as long as you were taking it; this is one cycle. Repeat it until you achieve your desired results.

Before using any supplements, always check with your doctor to make sure there will be no interactions with other prescription or over-the-counter medicines you may be taking.

When taking fat loss to the next level, you not only need to apply the principles you've learned about macro-patterning; you also need to understand how to use exercise in combination with a specific food plan to maximize results and make your body into a real fat-burning machine. I'll cover how to apply exercise efficiently in the next chapter.

2

Exercise Secrets to Maximize Fat Loss

Now that you understand the basics of the fat-loss code, let's take it to the next level. I'm going to show you how to melt fat more efficiently by exercising less. Many people assume that all exercise leads to fat loss, but do certain types of exercise do more? Just as foods are not created equal, neither is exercise. Experts and exercisers alike have missed the fact that the relationship between fat loss and exercise is a twofold process. Here's the secret!

Applying Exercise to a Specific Food Plan and the Importance of Timing

In this section, I'll show you what types of exercises to apply to the food plans I'll give you in Part 2. They say, "Timing is everything," and nowhere is that more appropriate than when it comes to setting up an exercise routine. This goes way beyond asking whether you are a morning, afternoon, or evening person. What I suggest here is something I refer to as a "fitness lifestyle," a philosophy that takes into account that the body is designed for balance. You can't just work out all you want and eat everything in sight or eat less because you don't exercise; to live a true fitness lifestyle and receive maximum health benefits while still losing fat, you need to achieve a balance between *how* you eat and *when* you move.

9

To get this balance, code crackers must understand that to lose fat efficiently they must apply exercise at the precise time based on their food intake. The real secret to diet and exercise is that fat loss needs the specific timing of exercise.

You may have read in other diet books that if you want to lose weight, you need to make sure you exercise to burn more calories than you consume. If you eat 500 calories, then go to the gym and run on the treadmill long enough to burn 500 calories, that equates to 0 calories. So no worries about storing fat, right? *Wrong!* This theory is incredibly flawed. Using a simple "calories in, calories out" equation fails to take into account the dynamic, challenging, and complicated systems of the human body. It also completely discounts the law of adaptation. That's right; you need to manipulate glycogen stores so they decrease.

The best part about manipulating your body's energy stores is that, ultimately, you can get it to store less fat altogether. When you manipulate glycogen stores over a long period of time, your body takes what it's eating and uses it to sustain energy levels—instead of storing it as fat. Remember when I explained how macro-patterning meal plans affect glycogen levels, forcing the body to melt fat? Well, applying certain types of exercises and timing them correctly will efficiently target those fat stores as well.

The secret is to include two types of exercise in your fitness regimen: aerobic (cardio) and anaerobic (weight training). Now we are going to look at how to apply exercise to your food plan and time your exercises so that you maximize your results by more than 80 percent. Just think, you'll actually have to exercise *less*!

The Two Types of Exercise: Aerobic and Anaerobic

Exercise is a broad term. People see someone working up a sweat and call it exercise, but what kind of exercise is it specifically? There are two types, and both have very specific benefits and rules when it comes to weight loss.

Aerobic Exercise

Aerobic literally means "with oxygen." Aerobic exercise, or *cardio*, is defined as activities in which oxygen from the blood is required to fuel the energy-producing mechanisms of muscle fibers. Examples are walking, running, cycling, and long-distance skiing. For purposes of fat loss, you will use cardio to produce heat and keep your metabolic fires burning.

Anaerobic Exercise

Anaerobic means "without oxygen." Anaerobic exercise, or weight training, is defined as highly intense, short-term activities in which muscle fibers derive contractile energy from stored internal compounds without using oxygen from the blood. Examples include short bursts of all-out effort, such as sprinting or weight lifting. Because anaerobic activity takes stored internal glycogen to produce the energy to generate movement, it is a valuable ally in your quest to lose weight.

Conquer the Code

An example of *aerobic exercise* is cardiovascular training. The purpose of this type of exercise is to produce heat in your body to keep your metabolism high.

Examples of *anaerobic exercise* are weight training and resistance training. The purpose of this type of exercise is to use internal energy stores—glycogen—for movement.

Understanding the Role of Cardio in Fat Loss

As I said earlier, cardio generates heat and higher metabolism. Doing cardio alone, however, doesn't necessarily equate to losing fat. This is definitely a misconception among many in the exercise community. Every year people make New Year's resolutions or anticipate special occasions where they want to wear something special, like a little black dress. This prompts them to start a weight-loss regimen, and what do they do? They immediately start walking or join aerobics classes because they think that will help them get rid of their excess weight. Sure, you *may* lose weight from doing lots of cardio, but is it really fat you're losing? Or could it be muscle tissue?

There has always been controversy over how much exercise the average human body really needs. Should you work out twice a week? Three times? Five times? Once a day? Twice a day? Even now experts are constantly updating their opinions as to what and how much is necessary, but I'm going to teach you the science of how to apply cardio—and, in the next section, weight lifting—to your food plan and use timing to maximize your results.

The Two Types of Cardio

There are two main types of cardio routines that are effective for fat loss: the high-intensity interval training (HIIT) method and the excess post-exercise oxygen consumption (EPOC) method.

High-Intensity Interval Training (HIIT)

This method consists of interspersing short bursts of quick-paced, high-intensity exercise within a less intensive cardio routine. An example would be alternating a minute-long sprint with several minutes of straight jogging or, for beginners, alternating a few minutes of jogging with several more minutes of brisk walking.

The HIIT method has recently become more popular in the media thanks to a flurry of research results that have shown its effectiveness when it comes to fat loss. This is encouraging because now more and more people are trying HIIT, but remember that fat loss is also dependent on *the levels of glycogen in your body.* When glycogen stores are low, HIIT can give you the most "bang for your buck."

You typically perform HIIT for fifteen to thirty minutes at a time. You burn the most calories while performing your chosen activity, such as alternating among sprinting, jogging, and brisk walking. In fact, recent research has shown that this method of exercise also keeps the metabolic rate sparked for longer periods of time even after the activity is over.

I suggest that clients use this type of training immediately after weight training to guarantee weight loss. Yes, I said, *guarantee!* Remember, weight training uses stored glycogen, so if you perform weight training and use your glycogen stores to provide your body with the necessary energy, then your stores will be low. If you perform cardio immediately *after* weight training, your stores are so low that your body will have to use excess fat stores to get the energy it needs to do your aerobic workout.

Let's put this in a practical application by applying HIIT to a meal plan. Let's say it's a carb-down day when your stores are already low, then you do some weight training followed by a cardio routine. Wow, talk about fat loss! To further ramp up the benefits of this already highly effective method, I also suggest when doing just cardio that you do your cardio using the HIIT first thing in the morning before eating anything.

How much should you do and when? Typically I suggest just fifteen to twenty minutes of HIIT first thing in the morning. To maximize fat loss, make it the morning after a carb-down day.

One of the most effective HIIT cardio sessions is something I call one-twos. You keep a quick pace for one minute, then follow it with two minutes at a slower pace; continue this pattern until your cardio routine is complete. You'll find more suggestions for using HIIT and EPOC later in this section.

Excess Post-Exercise Oxygen Consumption (EPOC)

This method is basically the opposite of HIIT; it consists of slow, long-duration cardio routines that typically last from 45 minutes to more than an hour. This type of cardio I like to use as my writing and planning cardio. I like the treadmill best for this method. I set the treadmill at a pace I can keep without holding on and a pace that will allow me to finish the time I am set to complete, and then I put my iPod on and listen to some music or books on tape and let my mind go. I kind of see the treadmill as meditative because the continued pace gets me almost in a mind-free state. In-line roller skating is great for this method as well. For clients who have more than 100 pounds to lose, I usually have them do this method on a recumbent bike because it puts less stress on the knees. For many years this was thought to be the preferred cardio method for fat loss because the body never enters an oxygen-deprived state, and fatty acids are guaranteed to be a main source of energy. Today there still is a lot of controversy over whether or not this method is the best way to burn fat. As I teach in my classes, fat loss is really based on the state of glycogen stores, so with that in mind, I suggest both methods of cardio for fat loss.

Which Type of Cardio Is Right for *You*?

Both HIIT and EPOC have been shown to be very effective in using up excess fat stores, as long as glycogen stores are manipulated to low levels (which is where the meal plans from Part 2 come in). So the decision of what method you use can really be based on the amount of time you have in your schedule.

I like to alternate the use of each method. For instance, in one month I might do two weeks of only HIIT and then follow that with two weeks of EPOC. To keep my body guessing, I might then use both methods for two weeks; for instance, do

HIIT in the morning after weight training and EPOC on the weekends any time of day.

Conquer the Code

If you're having trouble deciding which method is right for you, use the success tracker in Part 2 to keep notes about how you feel when you use HIIT and EPOC. Review this journal after a few weeks, and chances are you'll have positive emotions about one method or the other.

Why is variety so important? Why can't you simply get up in the morning, have a nice brisk walk, and not worry about it for the rest of the day? You can; unless your goal is fat loss. Going back to the 72/48 code from *Crack the Fat-Loss Code*, the body's forty-eight-hour response to exercise is the same as its response to food—it adapts to energy expenditure as well as energy intake. So changing your cardio routine is important to stop the body from trying to adapt.

Here is how I suggest using HIIT and EPOC together to maximize your losses:

• **If you have less than twenty-five pounds to lose:** For a healthy individual with only a slight to moderate weight problem, I suggest alternating the two methods as I described earlier. You might also decide which to use depending on the time of day when you're working out. First thing in the morning and immediately after a workout, HIIT is best. If you're exercising in the afternoon or early evening, use EPOC to keep your metabolic rate up.

• **If you have between twenty-five and a hundred pounds to lose:** In this case, I suggest going with EPOC alone to ensure the safety of sensitive joints and bones. However, you should still try to perform your cardio routine first thing in the morning or just after weight training.

• **If you have more than a hundred pounds to lose:** If you are in this category, I suggest using EPOC method and splitting your cardio routine working out for five to fifteen minutes at a time. Do this multiple times each day to raise your endurance and your metabolism.

Cardio is a key component for long-term success with significant weight loss, bringing it about both quickly and safely. I sometimes use this method for executives who complain that they have "no time" for aerobic exercise. In such cases, I break their routine into three periods throughout the day and suggest that they get a piece of equipment such as a treadmill or stair climber for their office. So when they get to work in the morning, they do ten minutes, then another ten minutes at lunchtime, and finally another ten minutes prior to going home. This way they still get their thirty minutes in, but the time is scheduled when it's available to them. Week to week, I change the pace up to stop their bodies from adapting.

Cardio Tips to Maximize Fat Loss

Here are some additional considerations for doing either type of aerobic workout to enhance your results and abide by the rules of the body's forty-eight-hour response:

• **You *must* exercise every forty-eight hours.** Do not go more than two days without exercising! Otherwise, your body will adapt and slow down your metabolic rate. As a helpful reminder, simply remember the part of the code that says your body responds to conserve energy every forty-eight hours.

• **Don't exercise the same way or for the same length of time more than ten days in a row.** Remember, your body is a calculator that is constantly trying to balance its internal checkbook, so once it has calculated what is coming in (food) and what is going out (energy), it adapts. When it does, that thirty-minute walk you take every day has the same effect as breathing in and out. So remember to change it up. Go farther, change your pace, and walk for a second time that day with your spouse or a friend. Whatever you do, don't let your exercise routine get stale; always keep it alternating.

• **Take one day off each week (or every fifth day).** If you dislike exercising, you can take every fifth day off; your body won't know, and your metabolism will continue to burn at the same rate. Using the "every fifth day" rule is better than always taking the same day off, because your body will get used to that too. Resting on different days is another way to prevent your body from adapting to your exercise regimen.

• **Never do cardio with resistance.** I see this drastic mistake at the gym all the time. People, especially women on a stair climber, add resistance, thinking, "Wow, my butt and legs are getting a hard workout." And they are, but the fact is this is a counterproductive way to perform aerobic exercise. In fact, this is a method of weight training called "time under tension," and it forces the body to store more glycogen—and possibly fat—in the lower half of your body, which actually makes your butt bigger. And that sure isn't the reason you're working out in the first place, right? So remember to use no resistance during cardio—only when weight training.

• **Whenever possible, do cardio first thing in the morning on an empty stomach.** Remember, this is the "prime time" for aerobic activity because glycogen stores are at their lowest and this is when fat loss is *guaranteed*.

Conquer the Code

Make sure your clothes are warm (or cool) enough and comfortable. Shorts that bind or leave a rash or a shirt that's too tight or too loose can be just one more excuse to keep you from exercising today.

Understanding the Role of Weight Training in Losing Fat

For years, weight training was popular among die-hard bodybuilders and gym fanatics. But only recently did the media and diet books begin introducing terms such as *resistance, curls,* and *free weights.* Women in particular are beginning to cozy up to the idea of actually lifting weights.

Today, of course, we recognize weight training—or building resistance—as one of the cornerstones of a successful fitness and weight-loss program. You've probably heard it countless times: the more muscle you have, the higher your metabolism will go, because for every pound of muscle on your body, you burn twenty to thirty calories, whereas for every pound of fat you carry, you burn only four to five calories. For that reason alone, many people have become weight-training enthusiasts! There are two basic methods of weight or resistance training:

- A high number of reps with light weights
- A low number of reps with heavy weights

When it comes to resistance training, the key is not to obsess about reps or weights but to reach the point of muscle fatigue. It doesn't matter whether you use lighter weights with a lot of reps or heavier weights with fewer reps; your body can't tell the difference. As long as the muscles you're working are tired, you're doing it right, because fatigue means you've stimulated the muscle. So if you're at the gym lifting light weights and counting out numerous reps, but you haven't fatigued the muscle, your exercise has had no effect on either that muscle or its use of glycogen.

For the maximum effect, you should use *both* methods of weight training and develop a weekly and monthly plan called *periodization.* As with cardio, this is a planned cycle of training in which you alternate types of workouts to stop your body from trying to adapt. It also helps keep things interesting—

and if you've ever lifted weights, you know that can become a real challenge when it's just you and the weight bench in the garage.

Burning Fat and the Weight-Training Connection

We talked about weight training becoming a part of any good fitness program and the role that fatigue plays in stimulating healthy muscle to burn more calories, but there is more to the connection between fat loss and pumping iron. Weight training is an anaerobic activity, and for your body to move anaerobically, it has to use stored internal compounds to supply the energy you need. And glycogen is that stored internal compound.

This is one of the most important aspects to fat loss, and in *Crack the Fat-Loss Code*, I mentioned five keys to efficient fat loss and optimal health. The first was to protect muscle. Rarely do diet books speak of weight training as the number-one key to fat loss, but science shows us a different reality. So if weight training uses glycogen to supply energy, does that mean there are better days to perform this type of exercise to lose more fat? The answer, of course, is *yes*.

Days when you are trying to lower your glycogen stores are the days when weight training will promote your efforts. For example, stores are lower on carb-down days because of the lower carbohydrate intake, so dipping into excess fat for energy is ensured. Later in this section we will identify the days when you should do weight training.

Weight-Training Tips to Maximize Fat Loss

Just as nutrition and cardio are important factors in weight loss, so is weight or resistance training. Its positive health benefits have made personal training a mainstream profession whose clientele is no longer just the rich and famous. Personal trainers can help anyone interested in learning the proper techniques for lifting weights.

Building muscle is complicated, and old-school beliefs about the best ways of doing it are obsolete. One example of this is the theory of how long you should train. It was once thought that the longer you worked out and the more reps and sets you did, the more muscle you would grow. Research has proven that this is incorrect because muscle-wasting hormones are released after weight training lasts fifty minutes to an hour.

Personal trainers not only teach you the proper techniques for using weights and machines, but they also motivate and push you to work harder and reach your goals. Even though I'm a personal trainer myself, when I'm training for a bodybuilding show, I hire a trainer for these very reasons. If hiring a personal trainer is just not in the budget, a wide variety of tapes are available for purchase or to rent. Or, join ForeverFit.com. Our site is striving to be one of the leaders for in-home personal training.

Here are some of my recommendations for using anaerobic activity in your fitness routine:

- Weight training should be performed at least twice a week. Do not exceed this without taking off every fourth day.
- If you are a beginner or just starting again, hire a professional for at least a few sessions to ensure your safety and understanding of proper techniques. Many gyms will provide a week pass to try out their gym, and they have personnel to show you how to use the machines. And of course don't forget about your local YMCA.
- Change your routine every few weeks to ensure your body doesn't adapt and stop your progress.
- Find a workout partner to help you stay motivated and ensure safety during sessions.
- Keep workouts under one hour so you won't trigger muscle-wasting hormones.
- Learn to have fun, relax, and make working out enjoyable.

I know, I know—you want more! The following section shows an example of how you might plan your cardio and weight-training routines based on what you have learned in this chapter. You should now understand how and why it is so important to plan and design your workout plans so fat loss is easy and guaranteed instead of exercising haphazardly for little or no benefit.

Sample Cardio and Weight-Training Plan for Macro-Patterning

Now that you know how important timing is to planning exercise on various meal plan days, let's put it all together so that we can take fat loss to an entirely new level.

The goal of exercise (for fat loss) is to reduce glycogen stores. Weight training should be done on days when you want to lower glycogen, such as carb-down days.

The following example has workouts on Tuesdays and Fridays to aid in reducing fat. An upper-body routine can be done on Tuesday and a lower body routine on Friday. The HIIT method of cardio is done on Wednesday and Saturday mornings because glycogen stores are at their lowest then. The EPOC method is used on Monday and Thursday afternoons or evenings because they fit into the schedule here. The format used here is similar to the one you will see in the training plans in Part 2 of this book.

DAY	MONDAY	TUESDAY	WEDNESDAY	THURSDAY	FRIDAY	SATURDAY	SUNDAY
Type day	Baseline	Carb down	Carb up	Baseline	Carb down	Carb up	Baseline
Workout days		Workout			Workout		Off
Cardio type	EPOC	HIIT	HIIT	EPOC	HIIT	HIIT	Off
Cardio amount	45–60 minutes	15–30 minutes	15–30 minutes	45–60 minutes	15–30 minutes	15–30 minutes	Off
Cardio time of day	Any time of day	After work or 1st in morning	1st in the morning	Any time of day	After work or 1st in morning	1st in the morning	Off

What to Eat Before and After You Exercise

One question I am often asked is, "When should I eat? Before or after I exercise?" First off, if you are diabetic, you should always have a small amount of protein prior to any exercise, be it cardio or weight training. This is important to keep your blood sugar levels balanced. For those who aren't diabetic, do morning cardio on an empty stomach and always eat immediately afterward because you will burn up the meal you are eating. Also, you will get more benefit from these meals if you eat proteins that need to be digested rather than whey-based proteins.

For afternoon and evening cardio sessions, you should wait thirty to sixty minutes before eating, because you will continue to burn fat during this time. If you are doing both cardio and weight training during the same workout, do your weight training first and always eat some protein before beginning. When you do both types of exercise together, sessions tend to be longer, and you don't want your body dipping into precious muscle tissue for energy.

Now that you have the tools you need to conquer the fat-loss code, let's put those tools into action. The next part of the book contains the actual nuts and bolts of specific meal cycles for eight weeks of fat burning and weight loss. You will also find daily meal plans and your success planner to log your progress. Let's get started!

What the Code Crackers Are Saying

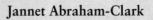

Jannet Abraham-Clark

I became the only female to make the Power Team, in 1990. The Power Team is a group of world-class athletes who use their talents to spread the gospel and inspire people around the world to make positive changes in their lives. They utilize visually explosive feats of strength, like breaking bricks and ripping phone books in half, to enthuse, astound, and inspire crowds from both the Christian and secular community. For years, I used being a weight lifter and power lifter, bench-pressing 345 pounds all natural, as my excuse to pack on the pounds.

I weighed 234 pounds with 32 percent body fat, but I figured, "Hey, I can bench-press 345!" Then one day I realized that I had climbed on that scale and it wasn't pretty. I had always wanted to enter a bodybuilding contest but could never discipline myself enough to diet. A bodybuilder friend of mine told me that I had a great build and would do well at a show. I thought, "Yeah, he's right. But how can I ever lose all of this extra weight?"

That's when I found Wendy Chant, a real live angel, to help me crack the fat-loss code. I followed the program from March 2006 until October of that same year and went from 234 pounds with 32

percent body fat to 178 pounds and 12 percent body fat; I took third place in my first-ever bodybuilding show. One month later, on November 4, I weighed in at 169 pounds (11 percent body fat) and was the runner-up in my second body-building show. I'm still using Wendy's program because I have realized that it's not just a diet, but a way of life!

PART 2

||||||||||||||||||||||||||

Your Success
Planner

3

How to Use Your Success Planner

What does it really mean to conquer the fat-loss code? You're about to find out! This section gives the real "meat and potatoes" of how you're going to reprogram your metabolism to melt fat and lose weight—forever. Here you will find your key to victory: the eight-week plan. The best part is the daily log sheets on which you mark your progress, failures, and lessons learned every twenty-four hours make the process interactive.

I have been teaching this plan in a classroom format and with clients one-on-one for more than eight years. Logging results is always one of the most important parts of the process, not just because it provides accountability, but because it also provides the raw data about what works best for each individual's body.

Your success planner consists of a target plan and a success tracker.

Your success planner has *every* base covered for you and with you. These aren't just casual recommendations, but specific, day-by-day plans that will take you through eight weeks of an intense fat-loss regimen. There will be no mystery about what to eat or which exercise is best depending on where you are in your program or what day of the week it is. I have spelled it all out for you.

How to Use Your Target Plan

Think of your target plan as a checklist for your day. I've designed it from top to bottom to resemble the best kind of daily planner: just start at the top each morning and work your way down:

• **Week:** Begin by making sure you're on the right week and recognizing what week it is (it's great when you can see how far you've come). This will help you stay focused, motivated, and on track.

• **Day:** Keeping track of your day helps you know how many days you've been successful and how far you have to go before reaching your ultimate weight-loss goals.

• **Cycle day:** There's no need to consult an appendix, an index, or a table of contents to know what type of day you'll be having. I've included this feature right at the top of the daily planner so you know what cycle day you're on.

• **Special reminders:** Before each meal plan you will find reminders of how much of a specific type of food you're supposed to eat that day and when.

• **A complete meal plan:** Each full meal plan is mapped out for you—every day for eight weeks! You may want to look at the week in advance to make sure you have enough raw materials for healthy eating on hand; this may also require extra evening or morning preparation if you have a busy day or week ahead of you.

• **Supplements:** I've inserted what supplements go with each day's menu and exercise plan to give you the best nutrition possible.

• **Exercise:** Each target plan includes the recommended daily dose(s) of exercise you'll need to catapult your fat loss to the next level. The suggested workouts appear where they should fall in your day (such as before breakfast or after your fourth meal) for maximum effect.

How to Use Your Success Tracker

Think of your tracker as a journal or day planner for success. However you think of it, it has been designed with you in mind. I know when my friends and I are busy and making lists or filling in blanks, we want enough room to write and we want all the blanks in the right places. Better yet, when I'm answering questions or making notes about something, I want that "something" readily available to compare and contrast.

How about side by side? This section is specifically designed so you can have both your daily target plan and your success tracker right next to each other so you can consult both as you move down the pages. As you look at your menu for a meal on one page, you can write in the time and what you actually ate on the next. If you fumble or fail or cheat, or have a breakthrough with a certain supplement or exercise, you can record it in the generous space provided. Simply go from one page to the next and you'll find them as compatible as they can be.

Your tracker has the following components:

• **Meal, drink, and snack log.** For each meal you will log in what you ate and when you ate it. This helps you see what kinds of foods you favor, when you get hungry naturally, and so on. Although it might not seem apparent in the first few days, once you're done with the first two weeks, you can flip through the pages and perhaps spot patterns that help you plan for and even avoid various cravings, temptations, or downfalls. You will also have a spot to log your water intake in eight-ounce quantities to help ensure that you are hydrated and that your body isn't storing carbs for hydration.

• **Supplements taken.** List the supplements you're taking here and any comments you may have, such as "The pills are too hard to swallow," or "I can really notice more comfort in my joints." By writing down your observations, you can decide which supplements are right and/or wrong for you.

• **Exercise.** This is the place to list your exercises and activities for the day.

• **How do you feel today?** This section allows you to reflect on your emotional and mental state for the day.

• **Describe your activity level.** Being honest here will really help you determine how comfortable you feel with various workout intensities—slow, leisurely, rapid, and intense phases. Over time, you should watch this entry carefully to see what changes have occurred and if you've been able to build your strength and endurance.

• **Did you have any food cravings? How did you manage?** I felt this section would be most helpful in detailing the powerful emotions that come along with food. By writing about your cravings and reflecting on your decisions or alternatives, you can begin to develop the willpower to avoid overeating as you continue with the program. I think you'll find this section one of your favorites on the tracker page!

Conquer the Code

Don't just scribble in your success trackers; actively *use* them. Mindlessly filling in the blanks or following directions feels too much like homework. Becoming an active part of your success requires you to really look at these pages and find a way to make them meaningful for you.

Overview of the Meal Plan Cycles

In this section, we meet your metabolism head-on and learn to outsmart it through cycles and meal plans. Whether you're a code-cracking pro or new to the game, here is an opportunity to make the next two months of your life your *best* two months!

We already know how the body is designed to find, gather, and store fat; we are literally fighting our own bodies when we try to lose fat. Well, the human body's been doing what comes naturally for thousands of years, so we're going to have to play some catch-up if we ever hope to beat it at its own game.

Advance meal planning is my answer. With these meal plans, there are many more options to keep your body from adapting. The fight is on! The plans I have designed use the science of how your body works and uses metabolic- and glycogen-manipulating foods to melt fat. Each of the three meal plan cycles over the next eight weeks was designed for specific results. The three cycles are as follows:

- Weeks 1–2: Double-Accelerated Fat-Loss Plan
- Weeks 3–5: Metabolic Increase Cycle (MIC)
- Weeks 6–8: Metabolic Adaptation Cycle (MAC)

As I explained earlier, within the eight-week cycles, there are specific cycle days that are patterned to prevent your body's adaptive response to food intake. Remember the codes for the individual days:

- **A** stands for deplete day.
- **B** stands for baseline day.
- **C** stands for carb-down day.
- **D** stands for carb-up day.
- **GF** stands for grapefruit day.
- **CH** stands for cheat day.
- **ZS** stands for zero starch day.

Along with each cycle day, you'll notice that I also code the type of meal you should be having. Each type of food has a specific key:

- **P** is for protein.
- **S** is for starch.
- **V** is for vegetable.
- **O** is for fat.
- **A** is for fruit.
- **SA** is for sweets and alcohol.
- **FF** is for free-food requirement.

For example, on a carb-down day (C), meal one is coded as P/S, which means that for this particular meal, you should have a protein and a starch. I've laid out the specific meal types in your daily meal plans. You'll also see the coded nutrient key in the substitution lists that I've provided, making it easier to follow the plan.

What the Code Crackers Are Saying

Sonja Smith

I started working out with Wendy and following her food plans after the birth of my first child eight and a half years ago. I was twenty-six years old, and I had never been happy with my body. After putting on fifty pounds during my pregnancy, I decided that I had to do something about my weight. Wendy gave me the knowl-edge, guidance, and support to not only lose the pregnancy weight, but more important, to maintain and keep the body I had always wanted. Within four months of starting to use the food plans Wendy created for me, I was a size 4 again.

Through her diet and exer-cise expertise, I was able to transform myself into someone I never believed was possible. I was able to get rid of body fat that I thought was part of my genetic makeup. I will be forever grateful to Wendy for helping me achieve my dreams and for creating a healthy lifestyle for me and my entire family.

4

Weeks 1–2:
Double-Accelerated Fat-Loss
Daily Success Planner

You might recognize the Double-Accelerated Fat-Loss Plan from the macro-patterning system we used in my first book, because the days are the same with a different arrangement. In the rules for the plan, I will give you a primer on the days and how they are organized to make your body an incredible fat-loss inferno. What makes this plan advanced is the double-up carb-down days, which are designed to keep glycogen stores lower to force your body to burn fat as a source of energy.

As you can see in the sample plan that follows, the Double-Accelerated Fat-Loss Plan includes three cycle days: carb-down, carb-up, and baseline days. The bulk of the cycle will consist of carb-down days, which will force your body's glycogen stores to drop drastically, maximizing fat loss.

• **Carb-down day (C).** We use the letter C for carb-down days; this letter system will help you locate recipes in Part 4 that will work on these days. This is the time to rely on your good friends "carbs" to help teach your body how to burn fat efficiently and to grab excess fat for energy. On carb-down days, your goal is to lower carbohydrate intake to reduce glycogen stored in your muscles so your body will have to rely on excess fat for energy when there is a deficit or need. Protein is still required at each meal, but you choose a starch source and have it at either breakfast or lunch. Fat intake should be limited to very little or none.

• **Carb-up or food-pass day (D).** We use the letter *D* for carb-up days. During these days you will use increased amounts of starches to spark your body's metabolic rate and provide it with nutrients for repair and growth. The last two meals on these days contain primarily carbohydrates. There are two carb-up days a week, and you'll notice that each immediately follows a carb-down day. My clients affectionately call these days their food passes; two days a week when you can let loose, splurge a little, and enjoy foods typically forbidden on other plans such as bread, dessert, pizza, and even alcohol. Keep the nutrients in the first few meals of the day similar to those for a carb-down day.

• **Baseline day (B).** We use the letter *B* for baseline days. As the name implies, you want to give your body a baseline to start from. On these days you basically just meet your body's immediate needs whenever it has them. Baseline days consist of basic nutrient intake, include proteins at each meal and one starch with breakfast and lunch, and limit fat intake to that from mostly "good" sources.

It's important to note the cycle day, because how you plan your meals will be affected by the type of day. For example, Monday is designated a carb-down day, where you can include a type of starch in a meal before 3 P.M. Although this may seem a bit complicated now, I promise that putting it all together will come easily once you start conquering the fat-loss code!

Double-Accelerated Fat-Loss Plan

WEEKS 1 AND 2

PLANNERS B, C, D	MONDAY DAY 1/8	TUESDAY DAY 2/9	WEDNESDAY DAY 3/10	THURSDAY DAY 4/11	FRIDAY DAY 5/12	SATURDAY DAY 6/13	SUNDAY DAY 7/14
Cycle day	C	C	D	C	C	D	B
Starch amount	1 × before 3 P.M.	1 × before 3 P.M.	Last 2 meals	1 × before 3 P.M.	1 × before 3 P.M.	Last 2 meals	2 × before 3 P.M.

Guidelines for Double-Accelerated Fat-Loss Plan

1. Eat every three to four hours up until two hours before going to bed.

2. You must have a minimum of four meals each day; five small meals are preferred.

3. Limit portions to the size of your fist. (When eating out, ask for a take-home container at the beginning of the meal and portion out your food.)

4. Drink at least your minimum water amount per day (70 to 80 ounces for women, 100 to 128 ounces for men).

5. Don't eat protein bars or fake, no-carb/low-carb prepackaged foods.

6. Alcohol and sweets maybe consumed on carb-up (D) days only.

7. Don't force meals or eat too much at each meal. The rule of thumb should be if you get to the next meal and you're not hungry, the meal before was too big; if you're starving before it is time to eat again, then the meal before was too small.

Substitution Food Lists for the Double-Accelerated Fat-Loss Plan

The following food substitution lists can be used for this cycle.

Type P = Protein Requirements and Substitutions

1. Consume protein at each meal, at least four times per day. Five meals are ideal.

2. Consume the amount of protein listed in the meal planner. An estimate is OK, but weighing your food after it is cooked is best. Remember that protein amounts are for cooked weight. When you order out, restaurants list the precooked weight on the menu, but meat cooks down by 1 or 2 ounces.

3. Cottage cheese may be consumed only once per day.

4. If you're consuming a protein shake, use a shake with 1 gram of sugar or less and carbs under 6 grams. Adjust the serving for not more than 25 grams (approximately 3 to 4 ounces) of protein for women and 40 grams (approximately 5 to 8 ounces) for men.

5. When eating egg whites, you may have one whole egg with your whites if desired.

6. Eat any of the following proteins.
    a. Egg whites or egg substitute
    b. Protein shake
    c. Cottage cheese
    d. Fresh fish: salmon, trout, and so on
    e. Lean beef
    f. Tuna
    g. Turkey breast
    h. Chicken breast

Type S = Starchy Carbohydrates Requirements and Substitutions

1. Consume *only* the following starchy carbs in the specified amounts.
   a. Oatmeal (½ cup dry measure)
   b. Potato, any kind (½ medium, 1 small, or 6 to 8 ounces)
   c. Cream of Rice or Wheat (1 serving per package label)
   d. Grits (1 serving per package label)
   e. Rice (½ cup cooked)
   f. Ezekiel bread—flourless bread or millet bread (2 slices)
   g. Black or red beans; lentils (½ cup cooked)

2. On carb-down days, consume one starch with a protein before 3 P.M.

3. On baseline days, consume two starches with a protein before 3 P.M.

Type V = Vegetable Requirements and Substitutions

1. You may consume any veggies *except for* carrots, corn, peas, or beets on carb-down or baseline days. You may consume carrots, corn, peas, or beets on carb-up days.

Type O = Fat Requirements and Substitutions

1. Consume the following good "a" fats before or instead of bad "b" fats (saturated or nonbeneficial fats) whenever possible.
   a. Flaxseed oil, olive oil, canola oil, essential fatty acid supplement
   b. Cheese, butter, mayonnaise, salad dressings, fatty red meat, sauces, and toppings

2. Limit the amount of fat you eat at meals containing starchy carbs.

Type A = Fruit Requirements and Substitutions

1. You may have one to two servings of any fruit on carb-up days.

Type SA = Sweets and Alcohol Requirements and Substitutions

1. If you have more than 30 pounds to lose, limit sweets and alcohol to help you reach your goal faster.

2. Limit alcohol consumption to one carb-up day per week for the best fat-loss results.

3. It is recommended that diabetics never consume alcohol.

4. The following are examples of the types of foods you can have for type SA.
   a. Pizza
   b. Pasta
   c. Bagels
   d. Crackers
   e. Breads

f. French fries

g. Chips and snacks

h. Corn, beets, or carrots

i. Ice cream

j. Alcohol

k. Sugary pastries

l. Cakes

Type FF = Free Food Requirements and Substitutions

1. Consume free food as a complement to a meal, not as a meal. (However, you can have flavored gelatin or a Fudgesicle as an evening snack on baseline days where indicated on your meal planner.) If hunger is an issue, choose a protein instead.

   a. Artificial sweetener

   b. Cooking spray

   c. Coffee

   d. Crystal Light drink

   e. Diet soda

   f. Hot sauce

   g. Lemon

   h. Lime

   i. Mustard

   j. Soy sauce

   k. Sugar-free tea

   l. Powdered spices

   m. Vinegar

   n. Worcestershire sauce

   o. Sugar-free gelatin (1 serving)

   p. Fudgesicle

Conquer the Code

Start to think of the days of the week as opportunities for your body to "grab fat." Don't merely follow the meal plan; learn to interpret why the days are arranged as they are and how you feel on each one. Later in this book, you will learn how to rearrange various meal plans or days of the week to prepare for weekends, holidays, special events, and even travel so that you never stop manipulating your body—instead of the other way around.

Sample Cardio and Weight-Training Plan for the Double-Accelerated Fat-Loss Plan

Based on the following example, anaerobic (weight-training) workouts are done on Monday, Tuesday, and Friday to help reduce glycogen stores. An upper body routine can be done on Monday, a lower body routine on Tuesday, and a full body workout on Friday.

The HIIT method of cardio is done first thing in the morning on Wednesday, Thursday, and Saturday, and in the afternoon on Monday, Tuesday, and Friday. Remember that only fifteen to thirty minutes is required for each cardio session.

DAY	MONDAY	TUESDAY	WEDNESDAY	THURSDAY	FRIDAY	SATURDAY	SUNDAY
Type day	Carb down	Carb down	Carb up	Carb down	Carb down	Carb up	Baseline
Weight-training days	Workout	Workout			Workout		Off
Cardio type	HIIT	HIIT	HIIT	HIIT	HIIT	HIIT	Off
Cardio amount	15–30 minutes	15–30 minutes	15–30 minutes	15–30 minutes	15–30 minutes	15–30 minutes	Off
Cardio time of day	1st in morning *or* after workout	1st in morning *or* after workout	1st in morning	1st in morning	1st in morning *or* after workout	1st in morning	Off

Target Plan: Week 1—Double Accelerated

DAY 1: Monday—Carb Down (C)

Carbs: 1 starchy carb at breakfast *or* lunch

ACTION	TYPE	WOMEN	MEN
Exercise		15–30 minutes HIIT	Weights (upper body routine) 15 minutes HIIT
Supplements		L-carnitine or lipotropic before workout	20 g protein powder mixed in water before workout; 1,000 mg vitamin C after workout
Meal 1	P/S	Protein Oatmeal (See Index.)	Protein Oatmeal (See Index.)
Supplements		Multivitamin and 1,000 mg vitamin C	Multivitamin and 1,000 mg vitamin C
Meal 2	P	½ cup cottage cheese	Chocolate shake: 30–40 g chocolate protein powder added to 10–12 oz. water in a blender; add ice for desired thickness and blend.
Meal 3	P/V/O	3–4 oz. grilled chicken on salad dressed with 1 tbsp. extra-virgin olive oil and vinegar	6–8 oz. grilled chicken on salad dressed with 1 tbsp. extra-virgin olive oil and vinegar
Meal 4	P	Chocolate raspberry shake: 20–25 g chocolate protein powder added to 10–12 oz. premade raspberry Crystal Light drink	Chocolate raspberry shake: 30–40 g chocolate protein powder added to 10–12 oz. premade raspberry Crystal Light drink
Exercise		Weights (upper body routine)	
Supplements		Lipotropic before workout; 1,000 mg vitamin C after	
Meal 5	P/V/V	6 oz. broiled halibut; 1 cup broccoli; small house salad with 1 tbsp. extra-virgin olive oil and vinegar	8 oz. broiled halibut; 1 cup broccoli; house salad with 1 tbsp. extra-virgin olive oil and vinegar
Supplements		Multivitamin and antioxidant	Multivitamin and anitoxidant
Meal 6	P	Egg White Poppers (See Index.)	Egg White Poppers (See Index.)

Notes: Women can do weights and cardio in the same session. Do weights first, then cardio. Men who have less than 20 pounds to lose don't need as much cardio. Men who want more muscle definition should do weights 3–5 days per week.

Success Tracker: Week 1—Double Accelerated

DAY 1: Monday—Carb Down (C)

Affirmation: "Life is a series of countless stages. I am open to the new and exciting times I will have exploring my path. I will welcome change."

Date: _____

Meals, Drinks, and Snacks

8 oz. water: ◯ ◯ ◯ ◯ ◯ ◯ ◯ ◯
◯ ◯ ◯ ◯ ◯ ◯ ◯ ◯

Breakfast: _____   Time: _____

Snack: _____   Time: _____

Lunch: _____   Time: _____

Snack: _____   Time: _____

Dinner: _____   Time: _____

Supplements Taken: _____

_____

_____

Exercise: _____

_____

_____

How do you feel today? _____

_____

_____

Describe your activity level: _____

_____

_____

Did you have any food cravings? How did you manage? _____

_____

_____

Target Plan: Week 1—Double Accelerated

DAY 2: Tuesday—Carb Down (C)

Carbs: 1 starchy carb at breakfast or lunch

ACTION	TYPE	WOMEN	MEN
Exercise		15–30 minutes HIIT	Weights (lower body routine); 15 minutes HIIT
Supplements		L-carnitine or lipotropic before workout	20 g protein powder mixed in water before workout; 1,000 mg vitamin C after workout
Meal 1	P/O	1 whole egg and 3 whites scrambled with sprinkle of cheese on top	1 whole egg and 5 whites scrambled with sprinkle of cheese on top
Supplements		Multivitamin and 1,000 mg vitamin C	Multivitamin and 1,000 mg vitamin C
Meal 2	P	Orange dream shake: 20–25 g protein powder added to 10–12 oz. premade orange-pineapple Crystal Light drink	Orange dream shake: 30–40 g protein powder added to 10–12 oz. premade orange-pineapple Crystal Light drink
Meal 3	P/S	3–4 oz. Spicy Cajun Chicken (See Index.); ½ cup rice	6–8 oz. Spicy Cajun Chicken (See Index.); 1 cup rice
Meal 4	P	Chocolate shake: 20–25 g chocolate protein powder added to 6–8 oz. water in a blender; add ice for desired thickness and blend.	Vanilla shake: 30–40 g vanilla protein powder added to 10–12 oz. water in a blender; add ice for desired thickness and blend.
Exercise		Weights (lower body routine)	
Supplements		Lipotropic before workout; 1,000 mg vitamin C after workout	
Meal 5	P/V/V	6 oz. turkey burgers; 1 cup broccoli; small house salad with 1 tbsp. extra-virgin olive oil and vinegar	8 oz. turkey burgers; 1 cup broccoli; house salad with 1 tbsp. extra-virgin olive oil and vinegar
Supplements		Multivitamin and antioxidant	Multivitamin and antioxidant
Meal 6	P	½ cup cottage cheese	1 cup cottage cheese

Notes: Women can do weights and cardio in the same session. Do weights first, then cardio. Men who have less than 20 pounds to lose don't need as much cardio. Men who want more muscle definition should do weights 3–5 days per week.

Success Tracker: Week 1—Double Accelerated

DAY 2: Tuesday—Carb Down (C)

Affirmation: "I face the challenges in my life, and I know I have unlimited resources available to me."

Date: _____

Meals, Drinks, and Snacks

8 oz. water: ○ ○ ○ ○ ○ ○ ○ ○
○ ○ ○ ○ ○ ○ ○ ○

Breakfast: _____   Time: _____

Snack: _____   Time: _____

Lunch: _____   Time: _____

Snack: _____   Time: _____

Dinner: _____   Time: _____

Supplements Taken: _____

_____

_____

Exercise: _____

_____

_____

How do you feel today? _____

_____

_____

Describe your activity level: _____

_____

_____

Did you have any food cravings? How did you manage? _____

_____

_____

Target Plan: Week 1—Double Accelerated

DAY 3: Wednesday—Carb Up (D)

Carbs: Last two meals predominantly starchy carbs, including sweets and alcohol

ACTION	TYPE	WOMEN	MEN
Exercise		15–30 minutes HIIT	15–30 minutes HIIT
Supplements		L-carnitine or lipotropic before workout	L-carnitine or lipotropic before workout
Meal 1	P/S	1 whole egg on ½ bagel	1 whole egg and 3 whites scrambled on ½ bagel
Supplements		Multivitamin and 1,000 mg vitamin C	Multivitamin and 1,000 mg vitamin C
Meal 2	P/O	Chocolate raspberry shake: 20–25 g chocolate protein powder added to 10–12 oz. premade raspberry Crystal Light drink	Chocolate raspberry shake: 30–40 g chocolate protein powder added to 10–12 oz. premade raspberry Crystal Light drink
Meal 3	P/S	3–4 oz. turkey breast with 1–2 slices cheese on 2 slices Ezekiel bread; small cup fruit	6–8 oz. turkey breast with 1–2 slices cheese on 2 slices Ezekiel bread; small cup fruit
Meal 4	SA	Chips and salsa (Don't stuff.)	Chips and salsa (Don't stuff.)
Supplements		Supplement containing chromium (such as Lean Out®)	Supplement containing chromium (such as Lean Out®)
Meal 5	SA	Plate of pasta with 1 meatball and marinara sauce; 1 small roll (Don't stuff.)	Plate of pasta with 1 meatball and marinara sauce; 1 small roll (Don't stuff.)
Supplements		Multivitamin, antioxidant, supplement containing chromium	Multivitamin, antioxidant, supplement containing chromium

Notes: Taking a supplement that contains chromium will help keep blood sugar levels lower, minimizing fat storage. We carry Lean Out at ForeverFit; it is manufactured by Beverly International. Use it to lower blood sugar and promote energy from food.

Success Tracker: Week 1—Double Accelerated

DAY 3: Wednesday—Carb Up (D)

Affirmation: "In my heart is a place of beauty and peace that nothing and no one can take away."

Date: _____

Meals, Drinks, and Snacks

8 oz. water: ◯ ◯ ◯ ◯ ◯ ◯ ◯ ◯
◯ ◯ ◯ ◯ ◯ ◯ ◯ ◯

Breakfast: _____   Time: _____

Snack: _____   Time: _____

Lunch: _____   Time: _____

Snack: _____   Time: _____

Dinner: _____   Time: _____

Supplements Taken: _____

_____

_____

Exercise: _____

_____

_____

How do you feel today? _____

_____

_____

Describe your activity level: _____

_____

_____

Did you have any food cravings? How did you manage? _____

_____

_____

Target Plan: Week 1—Double Accelerated

DAY 4: Thursday—Carb Down (C)

Carbs: 1 starchy carb at breakfast or lunch

ACTION	TYPE	WOMEN	MEN
Meal 1	P	Rolled Egg White Omelet with Mushrooms (See Index.)	Rolled Egg White Omelet with Mushrooms (See Index.)
Supplements		Multivitamin	Multivitamin
Meal 2	P/O	½ cup cottage cheese	1 cup cottage cheese
Meal 3	P/S	3-4 oz. tuna on Ezekiel bread; small side salad	6-8 oz. tuna on Ezekiel bread; small side salad
Meal 4	P	Mocha shake: 20-25 g chocolate protein powder added to 8 oz. water in a blender; add 1 heaping tsp. decaf or regular instant coffee and ice for desired thickness.	Mocha shake: 30-40 g chocolate protein powder added to 8 oz. water in a blender; add 1 heaping tsp. decaf or regular instant coffee and ice for desired thickness.
Exercise		45-60 minutes EPOC	45-60 minutes EPOC
Supplements		Lipotropic before workout; 1,000 mg vitamin C after workout	Lipotropic before workout; 1,000 mg vitamin C after workout
Meal 5	P/V/V	4-6 oz. Salmon Patties (See Index); 1 cup asparagus; dinner salad with vinaigrette dressing	8 oz. Salmon Patties (See Index); 1 cup asparagus; dinner salad with vinaigrette dressing
Supplements		Multivitamin and antioxidant	Multivitamin and antioxidant
Meal 6	P	Orange dream shake: 20-25 g protein powder added to 10-12 oz. premade orange-pineapple Crystal Light drink	Orange dream shake: 30-40 g protein powder added to 10-12 oz. premade orange-pineapple Crystal Light drink

Notes: Not a weight-training day. When doing EPOC—in a gym with cardio equipment or outside—keep a consistent pace. Men with less than 20 pounds to lose don't need as much cardio. Men who want more muscle definition should do weights 3-5 days per week.

Success Tracker: Week 1—Double Accelerated

DAY 4: Thursday—Carb Down (C)

Affirmation: "I see and attract to me others of a like fitness mind."

Date: _____

Meals, Drinks, and Snacks

8 oz. water: ○ ○ ○ ○ ○ ○ ○ ○
○ ○ ○ ○ ○ ○ ○ ○

Breakfast: _____ Time: _____

Snack: _____ Time: _____

Lunch: _____ Time: _____

Snack: _____ Time: _____

Dinner: _____ Time: _____

Supplements Taken: _____

_____

_____

Exercise: _____

_____

_____

How do you feel today? _____

_____

_____

Describe your activity level: _____

_____

_____

Did you have any food cravings? How did you manage? _____

_____

_____

Target Plan: Week 1—Double Accelerated

DAY 5: Friday—Carb Down (C)

Carbs: 1 starchy carb at breakfast *or* lunch

ACTION	TYPE	WOMEN	MEN
Exercise		Weights (full body routine); 15–30 minutes HIIT	Weights (full body routine); 15 minutes HIIT
Supplements		L-carnitine or lipotropic before workout; 1,000 mg vitamin C after workout	20 g protein powder mixed in water before workout; 1,000 mg vitamin C after workout
Meal 1	P/S/O	Egg Salad (See Index.) on 2 slices Ezekiel bread	Egg Salad (See Index.) on 2 slices Ezekiel bread
Supplements		Multivitamin	Multivitamin
Meal 2	P	2–3 oz. turkey breast rolled in lettuce	4–5 oz. turkey breast rolled in lettuce
Meal 3	P/V/O	Tomato stuffed with 3–4 oz. tuna; salad with cucumber, 1 tbsp. extra-virgin olive oil, and vinegar	Tomato stuffed with 6–8 oz. tuna; salad with cucumber, 1 tbsp. extra-virgin olive oil, and vinegar
Meal 4	P	Mocha shake: 20–25 g chocolate protein powder added to 8 oz. water in a blender; add 1 heaping tsp. decaf or regular instant coffee and ice for desired thickness.	Mocha shake: 30–40 g chocolate protein powder added to 8 oz. water in a blender; add 1 heaping tsp. decaf or regular instant coffee and ice for desired thickness.
Meal 5	P/V/V	Spicy Cajun Chicken (See Index.); 1 cup broccoli; small house salad with 1 tbsp. extra-virgin olive oil and vinegar	Spicy Cajun Chicken (See Index.); 1 cup broccoli; house salad with 1 tbsp. extra-virgin olive oil and vinegar
Supplements		Multivitamin and antioxidant	Multivitamin and antioxidant
Meal 6	P	Orange dream shake: 20–25 g protein powder added to 10–12 oz. premade orange-pineapple Crystal Light drink	Orange dream shake: 30–40 g protein powder added to 10–12 oz. premade orange-pineapple Crystal Light drink

Notes: Do weights first, then cardio. Men who have less than 20 pounds to lose don't need as much cardio. Men who want more muscle definition should do weights 3–5 days per week.

Success Tracker: Week 1—Double Accelerated

DAY 5: Friday—Carb Down (C)

Affirmation: "I'm strong and confident, and I love myself."

Date: _____

Meals, Drinks, and Snacks

8 oz. water: ○ ○ ○ ○ ○ ○ ○ ○
　　　　　　　　 ○ ○ ○ ○ ○ ○ ○ ○

Breakfast: _____   Time: _____

Snack: _____   Time: _____

Lunch: _____   Time: _____

Snack: _____   Time: _____

Dinner: _____   Time: _____

Supplements Taken: _____

_____

_____

Exercise: _____

_____

_____

How do you feel today? _____

_____

_____

Describe your activity level: _____

_____

_____

Did you have any food cravings? How did you manage? _____

_____

_____

Target Plan: Week 1—Double Accelerated

DAY 6: Saturday—Carb Up (D)

Carbs: Last two meals predominantly starchy carbs, including sweets and alcohol

ACTION	TYPE	WOMEN	MEN
Exercise		15–30 minutes HIIT	15–30 minutes HIIT
Supplements		L-carnitine or liptropic before workout	L-carnitine or lipotropic before workout
Meal 1	P/A	Super-Healthy Pancakes (See Index.) with side of berries	Super-Healthy Pancakes (See Index.) with side of berries
Supplements		Multivitamin and 1,000 mg vitamin C	Multivitamin and 1,000 mg vitamin C
Meal 2	P	Cinnamon Roll Smoothie (See Index.)	Cinnamon Roll Smoothie (See Index.)
Meal 3	P/O	Taco Salad (See Index.)	Taco Salad (See Index.)
Meal 4	SA	Chips and salsa (Don't stuff.)	Chips and salsa (Don't stuff.)
Supplements		Supplement containing chromium (such as Lean Out)	Supplement containing chromium (such as Lean Out)
Meal 5	SA	Seafood pasta; roll; 1 glass red wine; Simplest Fruit Cobbler (See Index.) (Don't stuff.)	Seafood pasta; roll; 1 lite beer; Simplest Fruit Cobbler (See Index.) (Don't stuff.)
Supplements		Multivitamin and antioxidant	Multivitamin and antioxidant

Notes: Do your cardio workout first thing in the morning because yesterday was a carb-down day. This morning is the best time for your body to use excess fat as an energy source. Do a full 30 minutes. Take a supplement that contains chromium to keep your blood sugar levels lower to minimize fat storage. We carry Lean Out at ForeverFit; it is manufactured by Beverly International. Use it to lower blood sugar and promote energy from food.

Success Tracker: Week 1—Double Accelerated

DAY 6: Saturday—Carb Up (D)

Affirmation: "I face challenges with a can-do attitude."

Date: _____

Meals, Drinks, and Snacks

8 oz. water: ○ ○ ○ ○ ○ ○ ○ ○
　　　　　　　 ○ ○ ○ ○ ○ ○ ○ ○

Breakfast: _____   Time: _____

Snack: _____   Time: _____

Lunch: _____   Time: _____

Snack: _____   Time: _____

Dinner: _____   Time: _____

Supplements Taken: _____

_____

_____

Exercise: _____

_____

_____

How do you feel today? _____

_____

_____

Describe your activity level: _____

_____

_____

Did you have any food cravings? How did you manage? _____

_____

_____

Target Plan: Week 1—Double Accelerated

DAY 7: Sunday—Baseline (B)

Carbs: 1 starchy carb at breakfast *and* lunch

ACTION	TYPE	WOMEN	MEN
Meal 1	P/S	Wendy's crepe: Mix together 3 egg whites, 1 scoop protein powder, ½ cup oatmeal, and ⅛ cup water for batter. Top with 1 serving sugar-free syrup or sugarless jam.	Wendy's crepe: Mix together 5 egg whites, 2 scoops protein powder, ¾ cup oatmeal, and ⅛ cup water for batter. Top with 1 serving sugar-free syrup or sugarless jam.
Supplements		Multivitamin	Multivitamin
Meal 2	P	½ cup cottage cheese	1 cup cottage cheese
Meal 3	P/S/V	3–4 oz. grilled chicken; ½ sweet potato; 1 cup steamed veggies	6–8 oz. grilled chicken; 1 sweet potato; 1 cup steamed veggies
Meal 4	P	Vanilla shake: Add 20–25 g vanilla protein powder to 10–12 oz. water in a blender; add ice for desired thickness and blend.	Vanilla shake: Add 30–40 g vanilla protein powder to 10–12 oz. water in a blender; add ice for desired thickness and blend.
Meal 5	P/V/V	4 oz. filet mignon; 1 cup asparagus; small house salad with 1 tbsp. extra-virgin olive oil and vinegar	6 oz. filet mignon; 1 cup asparagus; house salad with 1 tbsp. extra-virgin olive oil and vinegar
Supplements		Multivitamin and antioxidant	Multivitamin and antioxidant
Meal 6	P	Chocolate raspberry shake: 20–25 g chocolate protein powder added to 10–12 oz. premade raspberry Crystal Light drink	Chocolate raspberry shake: 30–40 g chocolate protein powder added to 10–12 oz. premade raspberry Crystal Light drink

Notes: Take this Sunday as a day off. Recovery is important to the entire body. Rest gives your body a chance to heal and rejuvenate. Don't underestimate the importance of a free day. In good weather, I like to use a day like this for other recreational activities like gardening or hiking. This is a great time to get the kids involved in fitness too.

Success Tracker: Week 1—Double Accelerated

DAY 7: Sunday—Baseline (B)

Affirmation: "Balance brings health, growth, love, and success."

Date: _____

Meals, Drinks, and Snacks

8 oz. water: ○ ○ ○ ○ ○ ○ ○ ○
○ ○ ○ ○ ○ ○ ○ ○

Breakfast: _____ Time: _____

Snack: _____ Time: _____

Lunch: _____ Time: _____

Snack: _____ Time: _____

Dinner: _____ Time: _____

Supplements Taken: _____

_____

_____

Exercise: _____

_____

_____

How do you feel today? _____

_____

_____

Describe your activity level: _____

_____

_____

Did you have any food cravings? How did you manage? _____

_____

_____

Target Plan: Week 2—Double Accelerated

DAY 8: Monday—Carb Down (C)

Carbs: 1 starchy carb at breakfast *or* lunch

ACTION	TYPE	WOMEN	MEN
Exercise		Weights (lower body routine); 15–30 minutes HIIT	Weights (lower body routine); 15 minutes HIIT
Supplements		L-carnitine or lipotropic before workout; 1,000 mg vitamin C after workout	20 g protein powder mixed in water before workout; 1,000 mg vitamin C after workout
Meal 1	P/O	Mocha shake: 20–25 g chocolate protein powder added to 8 oz. water in a blender; add 1 heaping tsp. decaf or regular instant coffee and ice for desired thickness.	Mocha shake: 30–40 g chocolate protein powder added to 8 oz. water in a blender; add 1 heaping tsp. decaf or regular instant coffee and ice for desired thickness.
Supplements		Multivitamin	Multivitamin
Meal 2	P	2–3 oz. turkey breast rolled in lettuce	4–5 oz. turkey breast rolled in lettuce
Meal 3	P/S/V	3–4 oz. grilled shrimp kabob; ½ cup rice; small house salad	6–8 oz. grilled shrimp kabob; ¾ cup rice; small house salad
Meal 4	P	Orange dream shake: 20–25 g protein powder added to 10–12 oz. premade orange-pineapple Crystal Light drink	Orange dream shake: 30–40 g protein powder added to 10–12 oz. premade orange-pineapple Crystal Light drink
Meal 5	P/V/V	Chicken Cacciatore (See Index.); Ballyhoo Zucchini (See Index.); spinach and mixed green salad with vinaigrette dressing	Chicken Cacciatore (See Index.); Ballyhoo Zucchini (See Index.); spinach and mixed green salad with vinaigrette dressing
Supplements		Multivitamin and antioxidant	Multivitamin and antioxidant
Meal 6	P	½ cup cottage cheese	1 cup cottage cheese

Notes: Women can split cardio and weight training into two different sessions. Do cardio first thing in the morning and weights later in the day. If you do both in the same session, do weights first, then cardio. Men who have less than 20 pounds to lose don't need as much cardio. Men who want more muscle definition should do weights 3–5 days per week.

Success Tracker: Week 2—Double Accelerated

DAY 8: Monday—Carb Down (C)

Affirmation: "I feel confident in expressing my feelings openly."

Date: _____

Meals, Drinks, and Snacks

8 oz. water: ○ ○ ○ ○ ○ ○ ○ ○
○ ○ ○ ○ ○ ○ ○ ○

Breakfast: _____ Time: _____

Snack: _____ Time: _____

Lunch: _____ Time: _____

Snack: _____ Time: _____

Dinner: _____ Time: _____

Supplements Taken: _____

_____

_____

Exercise: _____

_____

_____

How do you feel today? _____

_____

_____

Describe your activity level: _____

_____

_____

Did you have any food cravings? How did you manage? _____

_____

_____

Target Plan: Week 2—Double Accelerated

DAY 9: Tuesday—Carb Down (C)

Carbs: 1 starchy carb at breakfast or lunch

ACTION	TYPE	WOMEN	MEN
Exercise		15-30 minutes HIIT	Weights (upper body routine); 15 minutes HIIT
Supplements		L-carnitine or lipotropic before workout	20 g protein powder mixed in water before workout; 1,000 mg vitamin C after workout
Meal 1	P/S	Protein Oatmeal (See Index.)	Protein Oatmeal (See Index.)
Supplements		Multivitamin and 1,000 mg vitamin C	Multivitamin and 1,000 mg vitamin C
Meal 2	P	Chocolate shake: 20-25 g chocolate protein powder added to 6-8 oz. water in a blender; add ice for desired thickness and blend.	Vanilla shake: 30-40 g vanilla protein powder added to 10-12 oz. water in a blender; add ice for desired thickness and blend.
Meal 3	P/V	Egg Salad (See Index.) on baby spinach greens	Egg Salad (See Index.) on baby spinach greens
Meal 4	P	½ cup cottage cheese	1 cup cottage cheese
Exercise		Weights (upper body routine)	
Supplements		Lipotropic before workout; 1,000 mg vitamin C after workout	
Meal 5	P/V/V	Grilled seafood and veggie kabobs; small house salad with 1 tbsp. extra-virgin olive oil and vinegar	Grilled seafood and veggie kabobs; house salad with 1 tbsp. extra-virgin olive oil and vinegar
Supplements		Multivitamin and antioxidant	Multivitamin and antioxidant
Meal 6	P	Chocolate raspberry shake: 20-25 g chocolate protein powder added to 10-12 oz. premade raspberry Crystal Light drink	Chocolate raspberry shake: 30-40 g chocolate protein powder added to 10-12 oz. premade raspberry Crystal Light drink

Notes: Women can do weights and cardio in the same session if they choose. Make sure to do weights first, then cardio. Men who have less than 20 pounds to lose don't need as much cardio. Men who want more muscle definition should do weights 3-5 days per week.

Success Tracker: Week 2—Double Accelerated

DAY 9: Tuesday—Carb Down (C)

Affirmation: "I will let go of old patterns that restrict growth in my life."

Date: _____

Meals, Drinks, and Snacks

8 oz. water: ○ ○ ○ ○ ○ ○ ○ ○
⠀⠀⠀⠀⠀⠀⠀⠀○ ○ ○ ○ ○ ○ ○ ○

Breakfast: _____ Time: _____

Snack: _____ Time: _____

Lunch: _____ Time: _____

Snack: _____ Time: _____

Dinner: _____ Time: _____

Supplements Taken: _____

_____

_____

Exercise: _____

_____

_____

How do you feel today? _____

_____

_____

Describe your activity level: _____

_____

_____

Did you have any food cravings? How did you manage? _____

_____

_____

Target Plan: Week 2—Double Accelerated

DAY 10: Wednesday—Carb Up (D)

Carbs: Last two meals predominantly starchy carbs, including sweets and alcohol

ACTION	TYPE	WOMEN	MEN
Exercise		15–30 minutes HIIT	15–30 minutes HIIT
Supplements		L-carnitine or lipotropic before workout	L-carnitine or lipotropic before workout
Meal 1	P	Fake French Toast (See Index.)	Fake French Toast (See Index.)
Supplements		Multivitamin and 1,000 mg vitamin C	Multivitamin and 1,000 mg vitamin C
Meal 2	P/A	Chocolate Banana Protein Shake (See Index.)	Chocolate Banana Protein Shake (See Index.)
Meal 3	P/S	Five-Alarm Chili (See Index.)	Five-Alarm Chili (See Index.)
Meal 4	SA	Sushi rolls (Don't stuff.)	Sushi rolls (Don't stuff.)
Supplements		Supplement containing chromium (such as Lean Out)	Supplement containing chromium (such as Lean Out)
Meal 5	SA	Pizza; small dessert (Don't stuff.)	Pizza; small dessert (Don't stuff.)
Supplements		Multivitamin, antioxidant, and supplement containing chromium (such as Lean Out)	Multivitamin, antioxidant, and supplement containing chromium (such as Lean Out)

Notes: Take a supplement that contains chromium to keep your blood sugar levels lower, minimizing fat storage. We carry Lean Out at ForeverFit; it is manufactured by Beverly International. Use it to lower blood sugar and promote energy from the food. Do your cardio workout first thing in the morning because yesterday was a carb-down day. This morning is the best time to guarantee that your body will use excess fat as an energy source. Do a full 30 minutes.

Success Tracker: Week 2—Double Accelerated

DAY 10: Wednesday—Carb Up (D)

Affirmation: "I take time daily to reflect on my life and the positive path I'm taking."

Date: _____

Meals, Drinks, and Snacks

8 oz. water: ○ ○ ○ ○ ○ ○ ○ ○
○ ○ ○ ○ ○ ○ ○ ○

Breakfast: _____ Time: _____

Snack: _____ Time: _____

Lunch: _____ Time: _____

Snack: _____ Time: _____

Dinner: _____ Time: _____

Supplements Taken: _____

_____

_____

Exercise: _____

_____

_____

How do you feel today? _____

_____

_____

Describe your activity level: _____

_____

_____

Did you have any food cravings? How did you manage? _____

_____

_____

Target Plan: Week 2—Double Accelerated

DAY 11: Thursday—Carb Down (C)

Carbs: 1 starchy carb at breakfast *or* lunch

ACTION	TYPE	WOMEN	MEN
Meal 1	P/S	Wendy's crepe: Mix together 3 egg whites, 1 scoop protein powder, ½ cup oatmeal, and ⅛ cup water for batter. Top with 1 serving sugar-free syrup or sugarless jam.	Wendy's crepe: Mix together 5 egg whites, 2 scoops protein powder, ¾ cup oatmeal, and ⅛ cup water for batter. Top with 1 serving sugar-free syrup or sugarless jam.
Supplements		Multivitamin	Multivitamin
Meal 2	P/O	Chocolate raspberry shake: 20-25 g chocolate protein powder added to 10-12 oz. premade raspberry Crystal Light drink	Chocolate raspberry shake: 30-40 g chocolate protein powder added to 10-12 oz. premade raspberry Crystal Light drink
Meal 3	P/V	Tomato stuffed with 3-4 oz. tuna; small salad	Tomato stuffed with 6-8 oz. tuna; small salad
Meal 4	P	½ cup cottage cheese	1 cup cottage cheese
Exercise		45-60 minutes EPOC	45-60 minutes EPOC
Supplements		Lipotropic before workout; 1,000 mg vitamin C after workout	Lipotropic before workout; 1,000 mg vitamin C after workout
Meal 5	P/V/V	4-6 oz. rotisserie chicken; 1 cup steamed veggies; dinner salad with vinaigrette dressing	8 oz. rotisserie chicken; 1 cup steamed veggies; dinner salad with vinaigrette dressing
Supplements		Multivitamin and antioxidant	Multivitamin and antioxidant
Meal 6	P	Night scrambler: 1 whole egg and 2-3 whites scrambled and topped with salsa	Night scrambler: 1 whole egg and 4-5 whites scrambled and topped with salsa

Notes: This is not a weight-training day. When you're doing EPOC—in a gym with cardio equipment or outside—keep a consistent pace. Men who have less than 20 pounds to lose don't need as much cardio. Men who want more muscle definition should do weights 3-5 days per week.

Success Tracker: Week 2—Double Accelerated

DAY 11: Thursday—Carb Down (C)

Affirmation: "I learn and grow from life's experiences."

Date: _____

Meals, Drinks, and Snacks

8 oz. water: ○ ○ ○ ○ ○ ○ ○ ○
○ ○ ○ ○ ○ ○ ○ ○

Breakfast: _____ Time: _____

Snack: _____ Time: _____

Lunch: _____ Time: _____

Snack: _____ Time: _____

Dinner: _____ Time: _____

Supplements Taken: _____

_____

_____

Exercise: _____

_____

_____

How do you feel today? _____

_____

_____

Describe your activity level: _____

_____

_____

Did you have any food cravings? How did you manage? _____

_____

_____

Target Plan: Week 2—Double Accelerated

DAY 12: Friday—Carb Down (C)

Carbs: 1 starchy carb at breakfast *or* lunch

ACTION	TYPE	WOMEN	MEN
Exercise		Weights (full body routine); 15–30 minutes HIIT	Weights (full body routine); 15–30 minutes HIIT
Supplements		L-carnitine or lipotropic before workout; 1,000 mg vitamin C after workout	20 g protein powder mixed in water before workout; 1,000 mg vitamin C after workout
Meal 1	P/S/0	Protein Oatmeal (See Index.)	Protein Oatmeal (See Index.)
Supplements		Multivitamin	Multivitamin
Meal 2	P	Mocha shake: 20–25 g chocolate protein powder added to 8 oz. water in a blender; add 1 heaping tsp. decaf or regular instant coffee and ice for desired thickness.	Mocha shake: 30–40 g chocolate protein powder added to 8 oz. water in a blender; add 1 heaping tsp. decaf or regular instant coffee and ice for desired thickness.
Meal 3	P/V/0	3–4 oz. cold shrimp; salad with field greens, 1 tbsp. extra-virgin olive oil, and vinegar	6 oz. cold shrimp; salad with field greens, 1 tbsp. extra-virgin olive oil, and vinegar
Meal 4	P	2–3 oz. turkey breast rolled in lettuce	4–5 oz. turkey breast rolled in lettuce
Meal 5	P/V/V	Turkey Mishmash (See Index.); small house salad with 1 tbsp. extra-virgin olive oil and vinegar	Turkey Mishmash (See Index.); house salad with 1 tbsp. extra-virgin olive oil and vinegar
Supplements		Multivitamin and antioxidant	Multivitamin and antioxidant
Meal 6	P	Vanilla shake: Add 20–25 g vanilla protein powder to 10–12 oz. water in a blender; add ice for desired thickness and blend.	Vanilla shake: Add 30–40 g vanilla protein powder to 10–12 oz. water in a blender; add ice for desired thickness and blend.

Notes: Do weights first, then cardio. Men who have less than 20 pounds to lose don't need as much cardio. Men who want more muscle definition should do weights 3–5 days per week.

Success Tracker: Week 2—Double Accelerated

DAY 12: Friday—Carb Down (C)

Affirmation: "I love and appreciate my alone time."

Date: _____

Meals, Drinks, and Snacks

8 oz. water: ○ ○ ○ ○ ○ ○ ○ ○
               ○ ○ ○ ○ ○ ○ ○ ○

Breakfast: _____   Time: _____

Snack: _____   Time: _____

Lunch: _____   Time: _____

Snack: _____   Time: _____

Dinner: _____   Time: _____

Supplements Taken: _____

_____

_____

Exercise: _____

_____

_____

How do you feel today? _____

_____

_____

Describe your activity level: _____

_____

_____

Did you have any food cravings? How did you manage? _____

_____

_____

Target Plan: Week 2—Double Accelerated

DAY 13: Saturday—Carb Up (D)

Carbs: Last two meals predominantly starchy carbs, including sweets and alcohol

ACTION	TYPE	WOMEN	MEN
Exercise		15–30 minutes HIIT	15–30 minutes HIIT
Supplements		L-carnitine or lipotropic before workout	L-carnitine or lipotropic before workout
Meal 1	P/A	Low-Carb Pancakes (See Index.) with side of berries	Low-Carb Pancakes (See Index.) with side of berries
Supplements		Multivitamin and 1,000 mg vitamin C	Multivitamin and 1,000 mg vitamin C
Meal 2	P	Cinnamon Roll Smoothie (See Index.)	Cinnamon Roll Smoothie (See Index.)
Meal 3	P/O	Lentil Bean Soup (See Index.)	Lentil Bean Soup (See Index.)
Meal 4	SA	Fruit Smoothie (See Index.)	Fruit Smoothie (See Index.)
Supplements		Supplement containing chromium (such as Lean Out)	Supplement containing chromium (such as Lean Out)
Meal 5	SA	Tacos; make at home or go out and enjoy chips and salsa (Don't stuff.); 1 lite beer	Tacos; make at home or go out and enjoy chips and salsa (Don't stuff.); 1 lite beer
Supplements		Multivitamin, antioxidant, and supplement containing chromium (such as Lean Out)	Multivitamin, antioxidant, and supplement containing chromium (such as Lean Out)

Notes: Do your cardio workout first thing in the morning because yesterday was a carb-down day. This morning is the best time to guarantee that your body will use excess fat as an energy source. Do a full 30 minutes. Take a supplement that contains chromium to help keep your blood sugar levels lower, minimizing fat storage. We carry Lean Out at ForeverFit; it is manufactured by Beverly International. Use it to lower blood sugar and promote energy from food.

Success Tracker: Week 2—Double Accelerated

DAY 13: Saturday—Carb Up (D)

Affirmation: "I embrace the positive changes in my body."

Date: _____

Meals, Drinks, and Snacks

8 oz. water: ○ ○ ○ ○ ○ ○ ○ ○
             ○ ○ ○ ○ ○ ○ ○ ○

Breakfast: _____   Time: _____

Snack: _____   Time: _____

Lunch: _____   Time: _____

Snack: _____   Time: _____

Dinner: _____   Time: _____

Supplements Taken: _____

_____

_____

Exercise: _____

_____

_____

How do you feel today? _____

_____

_____

Describe your activity level: _____

_____

_____

Did you have any food cravings? How did you manage? _____

_____

_____

Target Plan: Week 2—Double Accelerated

DAY 14: Sunday—Baseline (B)

Carbs: 1 starchy carb at breakfast *and* lunch

ACTION	TYPE	WOMEN	MEN
Meal 1	P/S	1 whole egg and 2–3 whites scrambled; 2 slices Ezekiel toast	2 whole eggs and 3–4 whites scrambled; 2 slices Ezekiel toast
Supplements		Multivitamin	Multivitamin
Meal 2	P	½ cup cottage cheese	1 cup cottage cheese
Meal 3	P/S/V	3–4 oz. meat loaf; ½ baked potato; 1 cup steamed broccoli	6–8 oz. meat loaf; 1 baked potato; 1 cup steamed broccoli
Meal 4	P	2–3 oz. turkey breast rolled in lettuce	4–5 oz. turkey breast rolled in lettuce
Meal 5	P/V/V	4–6 oz. roasted turkey breast; 1 cup steamed veggies; small house salad with 1 tbsp. extra-virgin olive oil and vinegar	6–8 oz roasted turkey breast; 1 cup steamed veggies; house salad with 1 tbsp. extra-virgin olive oil and vinegar
Supplements		Multivitamin and antioxidant	Multivitamin and antioxidant
Meal 6	P	Orange dream shake: 20–25 g protein powder added to 10–12 oz. premade orange-pineapple Crystal Light drink	Orange dream shake: 30–40 g protein powder added to 10–12 oz. premade orange-pineapple Crystal Light drink

Notes: Take this Sunday as a day off. Recovery is important to the entire body. Rest gives your body a chance to heal and rejuvenate. Don't underestimate the importance of a free day. In good weather, I like to use this day to do other recreational activities like gardening or hiking. This is a great time to get the kids involved in fitness too.

Success Tracker: Week 2—Double Accelerated

DAY 14: Sunday—Baseline (B)

Affirmation: "I take positive action and work my plan daily."

Date: _____

Meals, Drinks, and Snacks

8 oz. water: ◯ ◯ ◯ ◯ ◯ ◯ ◯ ◯
◯ ◯ ◯ ◯ ◯ ◯ ◯ ◯

Breakfast: _____ Time: _____

Snack: _____ Time: _____

Lunch: _____ Time: _____

Snack: _____ Time: _____

Dinner: _____ Time: _____

Supplements Taken: _____

_____

_____

Exercise: _____

_____

_____

How do you feel today? _____

_____

_____

Describe your activity level: _____

_____

_____

Did you have any food cravings? How did you manage? _____

_____

_____

5

Weeks 3–5: Metabolic Increase Cycle (MIC) Daily Success Planner

The MIC, as I like to call it, is an advanced plan to help increase your metabolism. The secret to this cycle is based on the unique properties of grapefruit to spark your metabolic rate. The grapefruit diet is not a myth! With their high fiber content and low glycemic load, grapefruit may actually be secret weight-loss weapons.

The key to their effectiveness, however, is not to consume them daily and not to use this cycle for more than three weeks at a time. The real benefit we see in cycling grapefruit days into this plan is that new studies indicate a physiological link between grapefruit and insulin. The importance of this link lies in the hormone's weight-management function. While not its primary function, insulin helps regulate fat metabolism. Therefore, the smaller the insulin spike after a meal, the more efficiently the body processes food for use as energy and the less it stores as fat.

Remember that some prescription medications interact with grapefruit or grapefruit juice, so it is very important that you check with your doctor or pharmacist before beginning this cycle. If you are taking medication that prohibits grapefruit in your diet, you must abstain from grapefruit days. I've provided an alternative meal plan for MIC that includes zero starch days instead. Zero starch days are like deplete days, but you don't need to count carbs; you only have to abstain from eating the S and SA starches from the substitution list. Except for these, all vegetables consumed on a carb-down or baseline day are fine during this cycle.

The MIC includes three types of days: baseline days, grapefruit days, and carb-up days. Again, if you cannot consume grapefruit, I've included an alternative plan that replaces grapefruit days with zero starch days.

- **Baseline day (B).** We use the letter *B* for baseline days. As the name implies, you want to give your body a baseline to start from. On these days you basically just meet your body's immediate needs whenever it has them. Baseline days consist of basic nutrient intake, include proteins at each meal and one starch with breakfast and lunch, and limit fat intake to that from mostly "good" sources.

- **Grapefruit day (GF).** We use the designation *GF* for grapefruit days. On these days you will consume half a grapefruit during your first two meals. You may not use a substitute for the grapefruit (unless you need to use the zero starch plan for the entire day as already described). Protein is still required at each meal, and your fat intake should be limited to little or none.

- **Zero starch day (ZS).** We use the designation *ZS* for zero starch days. This is the time to rely on your good friends "carbs" to help teach your body how to burn fat efficiently and to grab excess fat for energy. On zero starch days, your goal is to lower carbohydrate intake to reduce glycogen stored in your muscles so your body will have to rely on excess fat for energy when there is a deficit or need. Protein is still required at each meal and you may eat plenty of veggies. You don't need to count carbs, although this day is similar to a deplete day, so you may have tomatoes on your salad and so on. Fat intake should be limited to very little or none.

- **Carb-up or food-pass day (D).** During these days you will use increased amounts of starches to spark your body's metabolic rate and provide it with nutrients for repair and growth. The last two meals on these days contain primarily carbohydrates.

Metabolic Increase Cycle

WEEKS 3 THROUGH 5

PLANNERS B, GF, D	MONDAY	TUESDAY	WEDNESDAY	THURSDAY	FRIDAY	SATURDAY	SUNDAY
	DAY 15/22/29	DAY 16/23/30	DAY 17/24/31	DAY 18/25/32	DAY 19/26/33	DAY 20/27/34	DAY 21/28/35
CYCLE DAY	GF	B	GF	B	GF	D	GF
Starch amount	½ GF first 2 meals	2 × before 3 P.M.	½ GF first 2 meals	2 × before 3 P.M.	½ GF first 2 meals	Last 2 meals	½ GF first 2 meals

Alternative Plan for Metabolic Increase Cycle

WEEKS 3 THROUGH 5

Grapefruit substitutions for this plan are listed in the notes section for each meal plan.

PLANNERS B, ZS, D	MONDAY	TUESDAY	WEDNESDAY	THURSDAY	FRIDAY	SATURDAY	SUNDAY
	DAY 15/22/29	DAY 16/23/30	DAY 17/24/31	DAY 18/25/32	DAY 19/26/33	DAY 20/27/34	DAY 21/28/35
CYCLE DAY	ZS	B	ZS	B	ZS	D	B
Starch amount	Zero starches	2 × before 3 P.M.	Zero starches	2 × before 3 P.M.	Zero starches	Last 2 meals	2 × before 3 P.M.

Guidelines for Metabolic Increase Cycle

1. Eat every three to four hours up until two hours before going to bed.

2. You must have a minimum of four meals each day; five small meals are preferred.

3. Limit portions to the size of your fist. (When eating out, ask for a take-home container at the beginning of the meal and portion out your food.)

4. Drink at least your minimum water amount per day (70 to 80 ounces for women, 100 to 128 ounces for men).

5. On grapefruit days, you must consume half a grapefruit or 4 to 6 ounces of no-sugar-added grapefruit juice. No substitutions are allowed.

6. If medication prevents you from eating grapefruit, zero starch substitutions are listed in the notes section for each meal plan.

7. Don't eat protein bars or fake, no-carb/low-carb prepackaged foods.

8. Alcohol and sweets maybe consumed on carb-up (D) days only.

9. Don't force meals or eat too much at each meal. The rule of thumb should be if you get to the next meal and you're not hungry, the meal before was too big; if you're starving before it is time to eat again, then the meal before was too small.

Substitution Food Lists for the Metabolic Increase Cycle

The following food substitution list is for the Metabolic Increase Cycle:

Type P = Protein Requirements and Substitutions

1. Consume protein at each meal, at least four times per day. Five meals are ideal.

2. Consume the amount of protein listed in the meal planner. An estimate is OK, but weighing your food after it is cooked is best. Remember that protein amounts are for cooked weight. When you order out, restaurants list the precooked weight on the menu, but meat cooks down by 1 or 2 ounces.

3. Cottage cheese may be consumed only once per day.

4. If you're consuming a protein shake, use a shake with 1 gram of sugar or less and carbs under 6 grams. Adjust the serving for not more than 25 grams (approximately 3 to 4 ounces) of protein for women and 40 grams (approximately 5 to 8 ounces) for men.

5. When eating egg whites, you may have one whole egg with your whites if desired.

6. Eat any of the following proteins.
   a. Egg whites or egg substitute
   b. Protein shake
   c. Cottage cheese
   d. Fresh fish: salmon, trout, and so on
   e. Lean beef
   f. Tuna
   g. Turkey breast
   h. Chicken breast

Type S = Starchy Carbohydrates Requirements and Substitutions

1. Consume *only* the following starchy carbs in the specified amounts.
   a. Oatmeal (½ cup dry measure)
   b. Potato, any kind (½ medium, 1 small, or 6 to 8 ounces)
   c. Cream of Rice or Wheat (1 serving per package label)
   d. Grits (1 serving per package label)
   e. Rice (½ cup cooked)
   f. Ezekiel bread—flourless bread or millet bread (2 slices)
   g. Black or red beans; lentils (½ cup cooked)

2. On carb-down days, consume one starch with a protein before 3 P.M.

3. On baseline days, consume two starches with a protein before 3 P.M.

Type V = Vegetable Requirements and Substitutions

1. You may consume any veggies *except for* carrots, corn, peas, or beets on grapefruit/zero starch or baseline days. You may consume carrots, corn, peas, or beets on carb-up days.

Type O = Fat Requirements and Substitutions

1. Consume the following good "a" fats before or instead of bad "b" fats (saturated or nonbeneficial fats) whenever possible.
   a. Flaxseed oil, olive oil, canola oil, essential fatty acid supplement
   b. Cheese, butter, mayonnaise, salad dressings, fatty red meat, sauces and toppings

2. Limit the amount of fat you eat at meals containing starchy carbs.

Type A = Fruit Requirements and Substitutions

1. You may have one to two servings of any fruit on carb-up days.

Type SA = Sweets and Alcohol Requirements and Substitutions

1. If you have more than 30 pounds to lose, limiting sweets and alcohol will help you reach your goal faster.

2. Limit alcohol consumption to one carb-up day per week for the best fat-loss results.

3. It is recommended that diabetics never consume alcohol.

4. The following are examples of the types of foods you can have for type SA.
   a. Pizza
   b. Pasta
   c. Bagels
   d. Crackers
   e. Breads
   f. French fries
   g. Chips and snacks
   h. Corn, beets, or carrots
   i. Ice cream
   j. Alcohol
   k. Sugary pastries
   l. Cakes

Type FF = Free Food Requirements and Substitutions

1. Consume free food as a complement to a meal, not as a meal. (However, you can have flavored gelatin or a Fudgesicle as an evening snack on baseline days where indicated on your meal planner.) If hunger is an issue, choose a protein instead.
   a. Artificial sweetener
   b. Cooking spray

c. Coffee

d. Crystal Light drink

e. Diet soda

f. Hot sauce

g. Lemon

h. Lime

i. Mustard

j. Soy sauce

k. Sugar-free tea

l. Powdered spices

m. Vinegar

n. Worcestershire sauce

o. Sugar-free gelatin (1 serving)

p. Fudgesicle

Sample Cardio and Weight-Training Plan for the Metabolic Increase Cycle

Based on the following example, workouts are done on Monday, Wednesday, and Friday to help reduce glycogen stores. This time, I'm suggesting that you split your upper body routine into separate sessions for big and small muscle groups, then do a lower body routine on the remaining day. An example would be to work on your chest, back, and abs on Monday; do a lower body routine on Wednesday; and work on your shoulders, arms, and abs on Friday.

Using HIIT cardio after workouts and on Saturday morning makes the most of your lowered glycogen stores. Use EPOC cardio any time on Tuesday and Sunday to keep your metabolism going. You can also switch Tuesday and Thursday every other week for days off if you wish. This same plan will work if you are using the alternative MIC meal plans (zero starch instead of grapefruit).

DAY	MONDAY	TUESDAY	WEDNESDAY	THURSDAY	FRIDAY	SATURDAY	SUNDAY
Type day	Grapefruit	Baseline	Grapefruit	Baseline	Grapefruit	Carb up	Baseline
Weight-training days	Workout		Workout		Workout		Off
Cardio type	HIIT	EPOC or switch with Thursday (off)	HIIT	Off or switch with Tuesday (EPOC)	HIIT	HIIT	EPOC
Cardio amount	15–30 minutes	45 minutes	15–30 minutes		15–30 minutes	15–30 minutes	60 minutes
Cardio time of day	1st in morning or after work	Anytime	1st in morning		1st in morning or after work	1st in morning	Anytime

Target Plan: Week 3—MIC

DAY 15: Monday—Grapefruit (GF)

Grapefruit: At first two meals

ACTION	TYPE	WOMEN	MEN
Exercise		Weights (chest, back, and abs); 15-30 minutes HIIT	Weights (chest, back, and abs); 15 minutes HIIT
Supplements		L-carnitine or lipotropic before workout; 1,000 mg vitamin C after workout	20 g protein powder mixed in water before workout; 1,000 mg vitamin C after workout
Meal 1	P/GF	Omelet made with 3-4 egg whites; ½ grapefruit	1 whole egg and 4 egg whites scrambled; ½ grapefruit
Supplements		Multivitamin	Multivitamin
Meal 2	P/GF	½ cup cottage cheese; ½ grapefruit	1 cup cottage cheese; ½ grapefruit
Meal 3	P/V/O	3-4 oz. grilled chicken on salad with 1 tbsp. extra-virgin olive oil and vinegar	6-8 oz. grilled chicken on salad with 1 tbsp. extra-virgin olive oil and vinegar
Meal 4	P	Chocolate raspberry shake: 20-25 g chocolate protein powder added to 10-12 oz. premade raspberry Crystal Light drink	Chocolate raspberry shake: 30-40 g chocolate protein powder added to 10-12 oz. premade raspberry Crystal Light drink
Meal 5	P/V/V	6 oz. broiled halibut; 1 cup asparagus; small house salad with 1 tbsp. extra-virgin olive oil and vinegar	8 oz. broiled halibut; 1 cup asparagus; house salad with 1 tbsp. extra-virgin olive oil and vinegar
Supplements		Multivitamin and antioxidant	Multivitamin and antioxidant
Meal 6	P	Orange dream shake: 20-25 g protein powder added to 10-12 oz. premade orange-pineapple Crystal Light drink	Orange dream shake: 30-40 g protein powder added to 10-12 oz. premade orange-pineapple Crystal Light drink

Notes: For the alternative plan, remove the grapefruit from meal 1 and add vegetables to the omelet; remove the grapefruit from meal 2. The rest of the day can remain the same. Do weights first, then cardio. Men who have less than 20 pounds to lose don't need as much cardio. Men who want more muscle definition should do weights 3-5 days per week.

Success Tracker: Week 3—MIC

DAY 15: Monday—Grapefruit (GF)

Affirmation: "When I exercise, I feel strong, confident, and refreshed."

Date: _____

Meals, Drinks, and Snacks

8 oz. water: ○ ○ ○ ○ ○ ○ ○ ○
○ ○ ○ ○ ○ ○ ○ ○

Breakfast: _____   Time: _____

Snack: _____   Time: _____

Lunch: _____   Time: _____

Snack: _____   Time: _____

Dinner: _____   Time: _____

Supplements Taken: _____

_____

_____

Exercise: _____

_____

_____

How do you feel today? _____

_____

_____

Describe your activity level: _____

_____

_____

Did you have any food cravings? How did you manage? _____

_____

_____

Target Plan: Week 3—MIC

DAY 16: Tuesday—Baseline (B)

Carbs: 1 starchy carb at breakfast *and* lunch

ACTION	TYPE	WOMEN	MEN
Meal 1	P/S	1 whole egg and 3 egg whites scrambled; 2 slices Ezekiel toast	2 whole eggs and 4 egg whites scrambled; 2 slices Ezekiel toast
Supplements		Multivitamin	Multivitamin
Meal 2	P	Crispy lettuce wrap: 2-3 oz. turkey breast and cheese rolled in fresh romaine leaves	Crispy lettuce wrap: 3-5 oz. turkey breast and cheese rolled in fresh romaine leaves
Meal 3	P/S/V	4 oz. tuna on 2 slices Ezekiel bread; small salad	6 oz. tuna on 2 slices Ezekiel bread; house salad
Meal 4	P	Vanilla shake: Add 20-25 g vanilla protein powder to 10-12 oz. water in a blender; add ice for desired thickness and blend.	Vanilla shake: Add 30-40 g vanilla protein powder to 10-12 oz. water in a blender; add ice for desired thickness and blend.
Exercise		45-60 minutes EPOC	45-60 minutes EPOC
Supplements		Lipotropic before workout; 1,000 mg vitamin C after workout	Lipotropic before workout; 1,000 mg vitamin C after workout
Meal 5	P/V/V	4 oz. filet mignon; 1 cup sautéed spinach; small house salad with 1 tbsp. extra-virgin olive oil and vinegar	6 oz. filet mignon; 1 cup sautéed spinach; house salad with 1 tbsp. extra-virgin olive oil and vinegar
Supplements		Multivitamin and antioxidant	Multivitamin and antioxidant
Meal 6	P	Chocolate raspberry shake: 20-25 g chocolate protein powder added to 10-12 oz. premade raspberry Crystal Light drink	Chocolate raspberry shake: 30-40 g chocolate protein powder added to 10-12 oz. premade raspberry Crystal Light drink

Notes: Not a weight-training day. When you're doing EPOC—in a gym with cardio equipment or outside—keep a consistent pace. Men who have less than 20 pounds to lose don't need as much cardio. Men who want more muscle definition should do weights 3-5 days per week.

Success Tracker: Week 3—MIC

DAY 16: Tuesday—Baseline (B)

Affirmation: "I use exercise as my 'me' time."

Date: _____

Meals, Drinks, and Snacks

8 oz. water: ○ ○ ○ ○ ○ ○ ○ ○
○ ○ ○ ○ ○ ○ ○ ○

Breakfast: _____   Time: _____

Snack: _____   Time: _____

Lunch: _____   Time: _____

Snack: _____   Time: _____

Dinner: _____   Time: _____

Supplements Taken: _____

_____

_____

Exercise: _____

_____

_____

How do you feel today? _____

_____

_____

Describe your activity level: _____

_____

_____

Did you have any food cravings? How did you manage? _____

_____

_____

Target Plan: Week 3—MIC

DAY 17: Wednesday—Grapefruit (GF)

Grapefruit: At first two meals

ACTION	TYPE	WOMEN	MEN
Exercise		Weights (lower body routine); 15–30 minutes HIIT	Weights (lower body routine); 15 minutes HIIT
Supplements		L-carnitine or lipotropic before workout; 1,000 mg vitamin C after workout	20 g protein powder mixed in water before workout; 1,000 mg vitamin C after workout
Meal 1	P/GF	½ cup cottage cheese; ½ grapefruit	1 cup cottage cheese; ½ grapefruit
Supplements		Multivitamin	Multivitamin
Meal 2	P/GF	Vanilla shake: Add 20–25 g vanilla protein powder to 10–12 oz. water in a blender; add ice for desired thickness and blend. 4 oz. grapefruit juice	Vanilla shake: Add 30–40 g vanilla protein powder to 10–12 oz. water in a blender; add ice for desired thickness and blend. 6 oz. grapefruit juice
Meal 3	P/V/O	3–4 oz. grilled chicken on salad with 1 tbsp. extra-virgin olive oil and vinegar	6–8 oz. grilled chicken on salad with 1 tbsp. extra-virgin olive oil and vinegar
Meal 4	P	Mocha shake: 20–25 g chocolate protein powder added to 8 oz. water in a blender; add 1 heaping tsp. decaf or regular instant coffee and ice for desired thickness.	Mocha shake: 30–40 g chocolate protein powder added to 8 oz. water in a blender; add 1 heaping tsp. decaf or regular instant coffee and ice for desired thickness.
Meal 5	P/V/V	6 oz. shrimp and scallop kabobs; 1 cup grilled eggplant and veggies small house salad with 1 tbsp. extra-virgin olive oil and vinegar	8 oz. shrimp and scallop kabobs; 2 cups grilled eggplant and veggies; house salad with 1 tbsp. extra-virgin olive oil and vinegar
Supplements		Multivitamin and antioxidant	Multivitamin and antioxidant
Meal 6	P	Orange dream shake: 20–25 g protein powder added to 10–12 oz. premade orange-pineapple Crystal Light drink	Orange dream shake: 30–40 g protein powder added to 10–12 oz. premade orange-pineapple Crystal Light drink

Notes: For the alternative plan, remove the grapefruit from meals 1 and 2. The rest of the day can remain the same. Do weights first then cardio. Men who have less than 20 pounds to lose don't need as much cardio. Men who want more muscle definition should do weights 3–5 days per week.

Success Tracker: Week 3—MIC

DAY 17: Wednesday—Grapefruit (GF)

Affirmation: "I work my plan one day at a time, and I give it 110 percent."

Date: _____

Meals, Drinks, and Snacks

8 oz. water: ○ ○ ○ ○ ○ ○ ○ ○
○ ○ ○ ○ ○ ○ ○ ○

Breakfast: _____   Time: _____

Snack: _____   Time: _____

Lunch: _____   Time: _____

Snack: _____   Time: _____

Dinner: _____   Time: _____

Supplements Taken: _____

_____

_____

Exercise: _____

_____

_____

How do you feel today? _____

_____

_____

Describe your activity level: _____

_____

_____

Did you have any food cravings? How did you manage? _____

_____

_____

Target Plan: Week 3—MIC

DAY 18: Thursday—Baseline (B)

Carbs: 1 starchy carb at breakfast *and* lunch

ACTION	TYPE	WOMEN	MEN
Meal 1	P/S	Wendy's crepe: Mix together 3 egg whites, 1 scoop protein powder, ½ cup oatmeal, and ⅛ cup water for batter. Top with 1 serving sugar-free syrup or sugarless jam.	Wendy's crepe: Mix together 5 egg whites, 2 scoops protein powder, ¾ cup oatmeal, and ⅛ cup water for batter. Top with 1 serving sugar-free syrup or sugarless jam.
Supplements		Multivitamin	Multivitamin
Meal 2	P	Mocha shake: 20–25 g chocolate protein powder added to 8 oz. water in a blender; add 1 heaping tsp. decaf or regular instant coffee and ice for desired thickness.	Mocha shake: 30–40 g chocolate protein powder added to 8 oz. water in a blender; add 1 heaping tsp. decaf or regular instant coffee and ice for desired thickness.
Meal 3	P/S/V	Five-Alarm Chili (See Index.)	Five-Alarm Chili (See Index.)
Meal 4	P	4 oz. shrimp cocktail	6 oz. shrimp cocktail
Meal 5	P/V/V	4 oz. chunk chicken on salad; Cabbage Soup (See Index.)	6 oz. chunk chicken on salad; Cabbage Soup (See Index.)
Supplements		Multivitamin and antioxidant	Multivitamin and antioxidant
Meal 6	P	Vanilla shake: Add 20–25 g vanilla protein powder to 10–12 oz. water in a blender; add ice for desired thickness and blend.	Vanilla shake: Add 30–40 g vanilla protein powder to 10–12 oz. water in a blender; add ice for desired thickness and blend.

Notes: This is not a weight-training day, so this week and next week you can switch your day off from today to Tuesday. Recovery is important to the entire body. Rest gives your body a chance to heal and rejuvenate. Don't underestimate the importance of a free day. In good weather, I like to do other recreational activities like gardening or hiking. This is a great time to get the kids involved in fitness too.

Success Tracker: Week 3—MIC

DAY 18: Thursday—Baseline (B)

Affirmation: "I trust change and embrace it."

Date: _____

Meals, Drinks, and Snacks

8 oz. water: ○ ○ ○ ○ ○ ○ ○ ○
○ ○ ○ ○ ○ ○ ○ ○

Breakfast: _____ Time: _____

Snack: _____ Time: _____

Lunch: _____ Time: _____

Snack: _____ Time: _____

Dinner: _____ Time: _____

Supplements Taken: _____

_____

_____

Exercise: _____

_____

_____

How do you feel today? _____

_____

_____

Describe your activity level: _____

_____

_____

Did you have any food cravings? How did you manage? _____

_____

_____

Target Plan: Week 3—MIC

DAY 19: Friday—Grapefruit (GF)

Grapefruit: At first two meals

ACTION	TYPE	WOMEN	MEN
Exercise		Weights (shoulders, arms, and abs); 15–30 minutes HIIT	Weights (shoulders, arms, and abs); 15–30 minutes HIIT
Supplements		L-carnitine or lipotropic before workout; 1,000 mg vitamin C after workout	20 g protein powder mixed in water before workout; 1,000 mg vitamin C after workout
Meal 1	P/GF	1 poached egg; ½ grapefruit	2 poached eggs; ½ grapefruit
Supplements		Multivitamin	Multivitamin
Meal 2	P/GF	Vanilla shake: 20–25 g vanilla protein powder added to 10–12 oz. water in a blender; add ice for desired thickness and blend. 4 oz. grapefruit juice	Vanilla shake: 30–40 g vanilla protein powder added to 10–12 oz. water in a blender; add ice for desired thickness and blend. 6 oz. grapefruit juice
Meal 3	P/V/O	Chef salad: 3–4 oz. deli meats and cheese, 1 whole hard-boiled egg, lettuce, and cucumber with 1 tbsp. extra-virgin olive oil and vinegar	Chef salad: 6 oz. deli meats and cheese, 2 whole hard-boiled eggs, lettuce, and cucumber with 1 tbsp. extra-virgin olive oil and vinegar
Meal 4	P	Orange dream shake: 20–25 g protein powder added to 10–12 oz. premade orange-pineapple Crystal Light drink	Orange dream shake: 30–40 g protein powder added to 10–12 oz. premade orange-pineapple Crystal Light drink
Meal 5	P/V/V	6 oz. turkey burger on portobello mushroom cap; 1 cup broccoli; small house salad with 1 tbsp. extra-virgin olive oil and vinegar	8 oz. turkey burger on portobello mushroom cap; 1 cup broccoli; house salad with 1 tbsp. extra-virgin olive oil and vinegar
Supplements		Multivitamin and antioxidant	Multivitamin and antioxidant
Meal 6	P	Chocolate raspberry shake: 20–25 g chocolate protein powder added to 10–12 oz. premade raspberry Crystal Light drink	Chocolate raspberry shake: 30–40 g chocolate protein powder added to 10–12 oz. premade raspberry Crystal Light drink

Notes: For the alternative plan, remove the grapefruit from meals 1 and 2. The rest of the day can remain the same. Do weights first, then cardio. Men who have less than 20 pounds to lose don't need as much cardio. Men who want more muscle definition should do weights 3–5 days per week.

Success Tracker: Week 3—MIC

DAY 19: Friday—Grapefruit (GF)

Affirmation: "I humbly express my gratitude and joy for my success."

Date: _____

Meals, Drinks, and Snacks

8 oz. water: ○ ○ ○ ○ ○ ○ ○ ○
○ ○ ○ ○ ○ ○ ○ ○

Breakfast: _____   Time: _____

Snack: _____   Time: _____

Lunch: _____   Time: _____

Snack: _____   Time: _____

Dinner: _____   Time: _____

Supplements Taken: _____

_____

_____

Exercise: _____

_____

_____

How do you feel today? _____

_____

_____

Describe your activity level: _____

_____

_____

Did you have any food cravings? How did you manage? _____

_____

_____

Target Plan: Week 3—MIC

DAY 20: Saturday—Carb Up (D)

Carbs: Last two meals predominantly starchy carbs, including sweets and alcohol

ACTION	TYPE	WOMEN	MEN
Exercise		15–30 minutes HIIT	15–30 minutes HIIT
Supplements		L-carnitine or lipotropic before workout	L-carnitine or lipotropic before workout
Meal 1	P/A	Fake French Toast (See Index.) with side of berries	Fake French Toast (See Index.) with side of berries
Supplements		Multivitamin and 1,000 mg vitamin C	Multivitamin and 1,000 mg vitamin C
Meal 2	P	Yogurt Smoothie (See Index.)	Yogurt Smoothie (See Index.)
Meal 3	P/O	Italian Roasted Pepper Soup (See Index.); crackers	Italian Roasted Pepper Soup (See Index.); crackers
Meal 4	SA	Popcorn	Popcorn
Supplements		Supplement containing chromium (such as Lean Out)	Supplement containing chromium (such as Lean Out)
Meal 5	SA	Pizza (Don't stuff.); 1 lite beer	Pizza (Don't stuff.); 1 lite beer
Supplements		Multivitamin, antioxidant, and supplement containing chromium (such as Lean Out)	Multivitamin, antioxidant, and supplement containing chromium (such as Lean Out)

Notes: Do your cardio workout first thing in the morning because yesterday was a carb-down day. This morning is the best time to guarantee that your body will use excess fat as an energy source. Do a full 30 minutes. Take a supplement containing chromium to help keep your blood sugar levels lower, minimizing fat storage. We carry Lean Out at ForeverFit; it is manufactured by Beverly International. Use it to lower blood sugar and promote energy from food.

Success Tracker: Week 3—MIC

DAY 20: Saturday—Carb Up (D)

Affirmation: "I speak from my heart and easily express my thoughts."

Date: _____

Meals, Drinks, and Snacks

8 oz. water: ○ ○ ○ ○ ○ ○ ○ ○
○ ○ ○ ○ ○ ○ ○ ○

Breakfast: _____ Time: _____

Snack: _____ Time: _____

Lunch: _____ Time: _____

Snack: _____ Time: _____

Dinner: _____ Time: _____

Supplements Taken: _____

_____

_____

Exercise: _____

_____

_____

How do you feel today? _____

_____

_____

Describe your activity level: _____

_____

_____

Did you have any food cravings? How did you manage? _____

_____

_____

Target Plan: Week 3—MIC

DAY 21: Sunday—Baseline (B)

Carbs: 1 starchy carb at breakfast *and* lunch

ACTION	TYPE	WOMEN	MEN
Meal 1	P/S	Protein Oatmeal (See Index.)	Protein Oatmeal (See Index.)
Supplements		Multivitamin	Multivitamin
Meal 2	P	Crispy lettuce wrap: 2–3 oz. turkey breast and cheese rolled in fresh romaine leaves	Crispy lettuce wrap: 3–5 oz. turkey breast and cheese rolled in fresh romaine leaves
Meal 3	P/S	Taco Salad (See Index.); ½ cup rice	Taco Salad (See Index.); 1 cup rice
Meal 4	P	Mocha shake: 20–25 g chocolate protein powder added to 8 oz. water in a blender; add 1 heaping tsp. decaf or regular instant coffee and ice for desired thickness.	Mocha shake: 30–40 g chocolate protein powder added to 8 oz. water in a blender; add 1 heaping tsp. decaf or regular instant coffee and ice for desired thickness.
Exercise		45–60 minutes EPOC	45–60 minutes EPOC
Supplements		Lipotropic before workout; 1,000 mg vitamin C after workout	Lipotropic before workout; 1,000 mg vitamin C after workout
Meal 5	P/V/V	4 oz. rotisserie chicken; 1 cup broccoli; small house salad with 1 tbsp. extra-virgin olive oil and vinegar	8 oz. rotisserie chicken; 1 cup broccoli; house salad with 1 tbsp. extra-virgin olive oil and vinegar
Supplements		Multivitamin and antioxidant	Multivitamin and antioxidant
Meal 6	P	Vanilla shake: Add 20–25 g vanilla protein powder to 10–12 oz. water in a blender; add ice for desired thickness and blend.	Vanilla shake: Add 30–40 g vanilla protein powder to 10–12 oz. water in a blender; add ice for desired thickness and blend.

Notes: Not a weight-training day. When you're doing EPOC—in a gym with cardio equipment or outside—keep a consistent pace. Men who have less than 20 pounds to lose don't need as much cardio. Men who want more muscle definition should do weights 3–5 days per week.

Success Tracker: Week 3—MIC

DAY 21: Sunday—Baseline (B)

Affirmation: "I focus on the positive things I do every day."

Date: _____

Meals, Drinks, and Snacks

8 oz. water: ○ ○ ○ ○ ○ ○ ○ ○
 ○ ○ ○ ○ ○ ○ ○ ○

Breakfast: _____ Time: _____

Snack: _____ Time: _____

Lunch: _____ Time: _____

Snack: _____ Time: _____

Dinner: _____ Time: _____

Supplements Taken: _____

_____

_____

Exercise: _____

_____

_____

How do you feel today? _____

_____

_____

Describe your activity level: _____

_____

_____

Did you have any food cravings? How did you manage? _____

_____

_____

Target Plan: Week 4—MIC

DAY 22: Monday—Grapefruit (GF)

Grapefruit: At first two meals

ACTION	TYPE	WOMEN	MEN
Exercise		15–30 minutes HIIT	Weights (chest, back, and abs); 15 minutes HIIT
Supplements		L-carnitine or lipotropic before workout	20 g protein powder mixed in water before workout; 1,000 mg vitamin C after workout
Meal 1	P/GF	Omelet made with 3–4 egg whites and spinach; ½ grapefruit	1 whole egg and 4 egg whites scrambled; ½ grapefruit
Supplements		Multivitamin	Multivitamin
Meal 2	P/GF	Vanilla shake: 20–25 g vanilla protein powder added to 10–12 oz. water in a blender; add ice for desired thickness and blend. 4 oz. grapefruit juice	Vanilla shake: 30–40 g vanilla protein powder added to 10–12 oz. water in a blender; add ice for desired thickness and blend. 6 oz. grapefruit juice
Meal 3	P/V/O	4–6 oz. roasted turkey breast; 1 cup steamed veggies; small house salad with 1 tbsp. extra-virgin olive oil and vinegar	6–8 oz. roasted turkey breast; 1 cup steamed veggies; house salad with 1 tbsp. extra-virgin olive oil and vinegar
Meal 4	P	½ cup cottage cheese	1 cup cottage cheese
Exercise		Weights (upper body routine)	
Supplements		Lipotropic before workout; 1,000 mg vitamin C after workout	
Meal 5	P/V/V	6 oz. broiled halibut; 1 cup asparagus; small house salad with 1 tbsp. extra-virgin olive oil and vinegar	8 oz. broiled halibut; 1 cup asparagus; house salad with 1 tbsp. extra-virgin olive oil and vinegar
Supplements		Multivitamin and antioxidant	Multivitamin and antioxidant
Meal 6	P	Chocolate raspberry shake: 20–25 g chocolate protein powder added to 10–12 oz. premade raspberry Crystal Light drink	Chocolate raspberry shake: 30–40 g chocolate protein powder added to 10–12 oz. premade raspberry Crystal Light drink

Notes: Alternately, remove the grapefruit from meals 1 and 2. Women can do weights and cardio in the same morning session. Do weights first, then cardio. Men who have less than 20 pounds to lose don't need as much cardio. Men who want more muscle definition should do weights 3–5 days per week.

Success Tracker: Week 4—MIC

DAY 22: Monday—Grapefruit (GF)

Affirmation: "I love my family and friends. We bring out the best in one another."

Date: _____

Meals, Drinks, and Snacks

8 oz. water: ○ ○ ○ ○ ○ ○ ○ ○
○ ○ ○ ○ ○ ○ ○ ○

Breakfast: _____ Time: _____

Snack: _____ Time: _____

Lunch: _____ Time: _____

Snack: _____ Time: _____

Dinner: _____ Time: _____

Supplements Taken: _____

_____

_____

Exercise: _____

_____

_____

How do you feel today? _____

_____

_____

Describe your activity level: _____

_____

_____

Did you have any food cravings? How did you manage? _____

_____

_____

Target Plan: Week 4—MIC

DAY 23: Tuesday—Baseline (B)

Carbs: 1 starchy carb at breakfast *and* lunch

ACTION	TYPE	WOMEN	MEN
Meal 1	P/S	Wendy's crepe: Mix together 3 egg whites, 1 scoop protein powder, ½ cup oatmeal, and ⅛ cup water for batter. Top with 1 serving sugar-free syrup or sugarless jam.	Wendy's crepe: Mix together 5 egg whites, 2 scoops protein powder, ¾ cup oatmeal, and ⅛ cup water for batter. Top with 1 serving sugar-free syrup or sugarless jam.
Supplements		Multivitamin	Multivitamin
Meal 2	P	Mocha shake: 20–25 g chocolate protein powder added to 8 oz. water in a blender; add 1 heaping tsp. decaf or regular instant coffee and ice for desired thickness.	Mocha shake: 30–40 g chocolate protein powder added to 8 oz. water in a blender; add 1 heaping tsp. decaf or regular instant coffee and ice for desired thickness.
Meal 3	P/S/V	Butternut Squash Soup (See Index.); small side salad with 3–4 oz. chunk tuna	Butternut Squash Soup (See Index.); small side salad with 6 oz. chunk tuna
Meal 4	P/O	Crispy lettuce wrap: 2–3 oz. turkey breast and cheese rolled in fresh romaine leaves	Crispy lettuce wrap: 3–5 oz. turkey breast and cheese rolled in fresh romaine leaves
Meal 5	P/V/V	4 oz. London broil; 1 cup sautéed spinach; small house salad with 1 tbsp. extra-virgin olive oil and vinegar	6 oz. London broil; 1 cup sautéed spinach; house salad with 1 tbsp. extra-virgin olive oil and vinegar
Supplements		Multivitamin and antioxidant	Multivitamin and antioxidant
Meal 6	P	Vanilla shake: Add 20–25 g vanilla protein powder to 10–12 oz. water in a blender; add ice for desired thickness and blend.	Vanilla shake: Add 30–40 g vanilla protein powder to 10–12 oz. water in a blender; add ice for desired thickness and blend.

Notes: Not a weight-training day; this week and next week you can switch days off with Thursday. Recovery is important to the entire body; rest gives the body a chance to heal and rejuvenate, so don't underestimate the importance of a day off. In good weather I like to use this time to do other recreational activities, and this is a great time to get the kids involved in fitness too.

Success Tracker: Week 4—MIC

DAY 23: Tuesday—Baseline (B)

Affirmation: "I deserve a healthy, beautiful body."

Date: _____

Meals, Drinks, and Snacks

8 oz. water: ○ ○ ○ ○ ○ ○ ○ ○
○ ○ ○ ○ ○ ○ ○ ○

Breakfast: _____ Time: _____

Snack: _____ Time: _____

Lunch: _____ Time: _____

Snack: _____ Time: _____

Dinner: _____ Time: _____

Supplements Taken: _____

_____

_____

Exercise: _____

_____

_____

How do you feel today? _____

_____

_____

Describe your activity level: _____

_____

_____

Did you have any food cravings? How did you manage? _____

_____

_____

Target Plan: Week 4—MIC

DAY 24: Wednesday—Grapefruit (GF)

Grapefruit: At first two meals

ACTION	TYPE	WOMEN	MEN
Exercise		Weights (lower body routine); 15–30 minutes HIIT	Weights (lower body routine); 15–30 minutes HIIT
Supplements		L-carnitine or lipotropic before workout; 1,000 mg vitamin C after workout	20 g protein powder mixed in water before workout; 1,000 mg vitamin C after workout
Meal 1	P/GF	3-4 oz. turkey and 1-2 slices cheese roll-up (roll turkey and cheese together and toothpick for a little on-the-go snack); grapefruit	5 oz. turkey and 2 slices cheese roll-up (roll turkey and cheese together and toothpick for a little on-the-go snack); grapefruit
Supplements		Multivitamin	Multivitamin
Meal 2	P/GF	½ cup cottage cheese; ½ grapefruit	1 cup cottage cheese; ½ grapefruit
Meal 3	P/V/O	6 oz. turkey burger on portobello mushroom cap; 1 cup broccoli; small house salad with 1 tbsp. extra-virgin olive oil and vinegar	8 oz. turkey burger on portobello mushroom cap; 1 cup broccoli; house salad with 1 tbsp. extra-virgin olive oil and vinegar
Meal 4	P	4 oz. shrimp cocktail	6 oz. shrimp cocktail
Meal 5	P/V/V	4-6 oz. roasted turkey breast; 1 cup steamed veggies; small house salad with 1 tbsp. extra-virgin olive oil and vinegar	6-8 oz. roasted turkey breast; 1 cup steamed veggies; house salad with 1 tbsp. extra-virgin olive oil and vinegar
Supplements		Multivitamin and antioxidant	Multivitamin and antioxidant
Meal 6	P	Chocolate raspberry shake: 20-25 g chocolate protein powder added to 10-12 oz. premade raspberry Crystal Light drink	Chocolate raspberry shake: 30-40 g chocolate protein powder added to 10-12 oz. premade raspberry Crystal Light drink

Notes: For the alternative plan, remove the grapefruit from meals 1 and 2. The rest of the day can remain the same. Do weights first, then cardio. Men who have less than 20 pounds to lose don't need as much cardio. Men who want more muscle definition should do weights 3–5 days per week.

Success Tracker: Week 4—MIC

DAY 24: Wednesday—Grapefruit (GF)

Affirmation: "I have the power to control my health."

Date: _____

Meals, Drinks, and Snacks

8 oz. water: ◯ ◯ ◯ ◯ ◯ ◯ ◯ ◯
◯ ◯ ◯ ◯ ◯ ◯ ◯ ◯

Breakfast: _____   Time: _____

Snack: _____   Time: _____

Lunch: _____   Time: _____

Snack: _____   Time: _____

Dinner: _____   Time: _____

Supplements Taken: _____

_____

_____

Exercise: _____

_____

_____

How do you feel today? _____

_____

_____

Describe your activity level: _____

_____

_____

Did you have any food cravings? How did you manage? _____

_____

_____

Target Plan: Week 4—MIC

DAY 25: Thursday—Baseline (B)

Carbs: 1 starchy carb at breakfast *and* lunch

ACTION	TYPE	WOMEN	MEN
Meal 1	P/S	1 whole egg and 3 egg whites scrambled; 2 slices Ezekiel toast	2 whole eggs and 4 egg whites scrambled; 2 slices Ezekiel toast
Supplements		Multivitamin	Multivitamin
Meal 2	P	Crispy lettuce wrap: 2–3 oz. turkey breast and cheese rolled in fresh romaine leaves	Crispy lettuce wrap: 3–5 oz. turkey breast and cheese rolled in fresh romaine leaves
Meal 3	P/S/V	4 oz. tuna on 2 slices Ezekiel bread; small salad	6 oz. tuna on 2 slices Ezekiel bread; salad
Meal 4	P	Vanilla shake: Add 20–25 g vanilla protein powder to 10–12 oz. water in a blender; add ice for desired thickness and blend.	Vanilla shake: Add 30–40 g vanilla protein powder to 10–12 oz. water in a blender; add ice for desired thickness and blend.
Exercise		45–60 minutes EPOC	45–60 minutes EPOC
Supplements		Lipotropic before workout; 1,000 mg vitamin C after workout	Lipotropic before workout; 1,000 mg vitamin C after workout
Meal 5	P/V/V	4 oz. filet mignon; 1 cup sautéed spinach; small house salad with 1 tbsp. extra-virgin olive oil and vinegar	6 oz. filet mignon; 1 cup sautéed spinach; house salad with 1 tbsp. extra-virgin olive oil and vinegar
Supplements		Multivitamin and antioxidant	Multivitamin and antioxidant
Meal 6	P	Chocolate raspberry shake: 20–25 g chocolate protein powder added to 10–12 oz. premade raspberry Crystal Light drink	Chocolate raspberry shake: 30–40 g chocolate protein powder added to 10–12 oz. premade raspberry Crystal Light drink

Notes: Not a weight-training day. When you're doing EPOC—in a gym with cardio equipment or outside—keep a consistent pace. Men who have less than 20 pounds to lose don't need as much cardio. Men who want more muscle definition should do weights 3–5 days per week.

Success Tracker: Week 4—MIC

DAY 25: Thursday—Baseline (B)

Affirmation: "I am filled with energy to do all the daily activities in my life."

Date: _____

Meals, Drinks, and Snacks

8 oz. water: ◯ ◯ ◯ ◯ ◯ ◯ ◯ ◯
◯ ◯ ◯ ◯ ◯ ◯ ◯ ◯

Breakfast: _____ Time: _____

Snack: _____ Time: _____

Lunch: _____ Time: _____

Snack: _____ Time: _____

Dinner: _____ Time: _____

Supplements Taken: _____

_____

_____

Exercise: _____

_____

_____

How do you feel today? _____

_____

_____

Describe your activity level: _____

_____

_____

Did you have any food cravings? How did you manage? _____

_____

_____

Target Plan: Week 4—MIC

DAY 26: Friday—Grapefruit (GF)

Grapefruit: At first two meals

ACTION	TYPE	WOMEN	MEN
Exercise		Weights (shoulders, arms, and abs); 15–30 minutes HIIT	Weights (shoulders, arms, and abs); 15–30 minutes HIIT
Supplements		L-carnitine or lipotropic before workout; 1,000 mg vitamin C after workout	20 g protein powder mixed in water before workout; 1,000 mg vitamin C after workout
Meal 1	P/GF	1 whole egg and 3 egg whites scrambled; ½ grapefruit	2 whole eggs and 4 egg whites scrambled; ½ grapefruit
Supplements		Multivitamin	Multivitamin
Meal 2	P/GF	Vanilla shake: 20–25 g vanilla protein powder added to 10–12 oz. water in a blender; add ice for desired thickness and blend. 4 oz. grapefruit juice	Vanilla shake: 30–40 g vanilla protein powder added to 10–12 oz. water in a blender; add ice for desired thickness and blend. 6 oz. grapefruit juice
Meal 3	P/V/O	3–4 oz. cold shrimp; salad with field greens, 1 tbsp. extra-virgin olive oil, and vinegar	6 oz. cold shrimp; salad with field greens, 1 tbsp. extra-virgin olive oil, and vinegar
Meal 4	P	2–3 oz. turkey breast rolled in lettuce	4–5 oz. turkey breast rolled in lettuce
Meal 5	P/V/V	6 oz. broiled salmon; 1 cup asparagus; small house salad with 1 tbsp. extra-virgin olive oil and vinegar	8 oz. broiled salmon; 1 cup asparagus; house salad with 1 tbsp. extra-virgin olive oil and vinegar
Supplements		Multivitamin and antioxidant	Multivitamin and antioxidant
Meal 6	P	Orange dream shake: 20–25 g protein powder added to 10–12 oz. premade orange-pineapple Crystal Light drink	Orange dream shake: 30–40 g protein powder added to 10–12 oz. premade orange-pineapple Crystal Light drink

Notes: For the alternative plan, remove the grapefruit from meals 1 and 2. The rest of the day can remain the same. Women can do weights and cardio in the same session if they choose. Do weights first, then cardio. Men who have less than 20 pounds to lose don't need as much cardio. Men who want more muscle definition should do weights 3–5 days per week.

Success Tracker: Week 4—MIC

DAY 26: Friday—Grapefruit (GF)

Affirmation: "I love and care for my body, and it cares for me."

Date: _____

Meals, Drinks, and Snacks

8 oz. water: ○ ○ ○ ○ ○ ○ ○ ○
○ ○ ○ ○ ○ ○ ○ ○

Breakfast: _____ Time: _____

Snack: _____ Time: _____

Lunch: _____ Time: _____

Snack: _____ Time: _____

Dinner: _____ Time: _____

Supplements Taken: _____

_____

_____

Exercise: _____

_____

_____

How do you feel today? _____

_____

_____

Describe your activity level: _____

_____

_____

Did you have any food cravings? How did you manage? _____

_____

_____

Target Plan: Week 4—MIC

DAY 27: Saturday—Carb Up (D)

Carbs: Last two meals predominantly starchy carbs, including sweets and alcohol

ACTION	TYPE	WOMEN	MEN
Exercise		30 minutes HIIT	30 minutes HIIT
Supplements		L-carnitine or lipotropic before workout	L-carnitine or lipotropic before workout
Meal 1	P/A	Chocolate Banana Protein Shake (See Index.)	Chocolate Banana Protein Shake (See Index.)
Supplements		Multivitamin and 1,000 mg vitamin C	Multivitamin and 1,000 mg vitamin C
Meal 2	P/S	Egg bagel: 1 whole egg and 2-3 egg whites scrambled, on ½ bagel	Egg bagel: 1 whole egg and 4-5 whites scrambled, on 1 bagel
Meal 3	P/S/O	6" roast beef and Swiss sub sandwich on wheat bread; small bag of chips	6" roast beef and Swiss sub sandwich on wheat bread; small bag of chips
Meal 4	SA	Popcorn	Popcorn
Supplements		Supplement containing chromium (such as Lean Out)	Supplement containing chromium (such as Lean Out)
Meal 5	SA	Herbed chicken penne pasta (use a family recipe or enjoy out at your favorite restaurant); crusty roll (Don't stuff.)	Herbed chicken penne pasta (use a family recipe or enjoy out at your favorite restaurant); crusty roll (Don't stuff.)
Supplements		Multivitamin and antioxidant	Multivitamin and antioxidant

Notes: Do your cardio workout first thing in the morning because yesterday was a carb-down day. This morning is the best time to guarantee that your body will use excess fat as an energy source. Do a full 30 minutes. Take a supplement that contains chromium to help keep your blood sugar levels lower, minimizing fat storage. We carry Lean Out at ForeverFit; it is manufactured by Beverly International. Use it to lower blood sugar and promote energy from food.

Success Tracker: Week 4—MIC

DAY 27: Saturday—Carb Up (D)

Affirmation: "I am a success in all that I do."

Date: _____

Meals, Drinks, and Snacks

8 oz. water: ○ ○ ○ ○ ○ ○ ○ ○
○ ○ ○ ○ ○ ○ ○ ○

Breakfast: _____   Time: _____

Snack: _____   Time: _____

Lunch: _____   Time: _____

Snack: _____   Time: _____

Dinner: _____   Time: _____

Supplements Taken: _____

_____

_____

Exercise: _____

_____

_____

How do you feel today? _____

_____

_____

Describe your activity level: _____

_____

_____

Did you have any food cravings? How did you manage? _____

_____

_____

Target Plan: Week 4—MIC

DAY 28: Sunday—Baseline (B)

Carbs: 1 stacarb at breakfast *and* lunch

ACTION	TYPE	WOMEN	MEN
Meal 1	P/S	Protein Oatmeal (See Index.)	Protein Oatmeal (See Index.)
Supplements		Multivitamin	Multivitamin
Meal 2	P	Crispy lettuce wrap: 2-3 oz. turkey breast and cheese rolled in fresh romaine leaves	Crispy lettuce wrap: 3-5 oz. turkey breast and cheese rolled in fresh romaine leaves
Meal 3	P/S	Taco Salad (See Index.); ½ cup rice	Taco Salad (See Index.); 1 cup rice
Meal 4	P	Mocha shake: 20-25 g chocolate protein powder added to 8 oz. water in a blender; add 1 heaping tsp. decaf or regular instant coffee and ice for desired thickness.	Mocha shake: 30-40 g chocolate protein powder added to 8 oz. water in a blender; add 1 heaping tsp. decaf or regular instant coffee and ice for desired thickness.
Exercise		45-60 minutes EPOC	45-60 minutes EPOC
Supplements		Lipotropic before workout; 1,000 mg vitamin C after workout	Lipotropic before workout; 1,000 mg vitamin C after workout
Meal 5	P/V/V	6 oz. shrimp and scallop kabobs; grilled eggplant and veggies; small house salad with 1 tbsp. extra-virgin olive oil and vinegar	8 oz. shrimp and scallop kabobs; grilled eggplant and veggies; house salad with 1 tbsp. extra-virgin olive oil and vinegar
Supplements		Multivitamin and antioxidant	Multivitamin and antioxidant
Meal 6	P	Orange dream shake: 20-25 g protein powder added to 10-12 oz. premade orange-pineapple Crystal Light drink	Orange dream shake: 30-40 g protein powder added to 10-12 oz. premade orange-pineapple Crystal Light drink

Notes: Not a weight-training day. When you're doing EPOC—in a gym with cardio equipment or outside—keep a consistent pace. Men who have less than 20 pounds to lose don't need as much cardio. Men who want more muscle definition should do weights 3-5 days per week.

Success Tracker: Week 4—MIC

DAY 28: Sunday—Baseline (B)

Affirmation: "Plans never fail. People fail to plan, so for success, work your plan."

Date: _____

Meals, Drinks, and Snacks

8 oz. water: ○ ○ ○ ○ ○ ○ ○ ○
              ○ ○ ○ ○ ○ ○ ○ ○

Breakfast: _____ Time: _____

Snack: _____ Time: _____

Lunch: _____ Time: _____

Snack: _____ Time: _____

Dinner: _____ Time: _____

Supplements Taken: _____

_____

_____

Exercise: _____

_____

_____

How do you feel today? _____

_____

_____

Describe your activity level: _____

_____

_____

Did you have any food cravings? How did you manage? _____

_____

_____

Target Plan: Week 5—MIC

DAY 29: Monday—Grapefruit (GF)

Grapefruit: At first two meals

ACTION	TYPE	WOMEN	MEN
Exercise		Weights (chest, back, and abs); 15–30 minutes HIIT	Weights (chest, back, and abs); 15–30 minutes HIIT
Supplements		L-carnitine or lipotropic before workout; 1,000 mg vitamin C after workout	20 g protein powder mixed in water before workout; 1,000 mg vitamin C after workout
Meal 1	P/GF	Omelet made with 3–4 egg whites; ½ grapefruit	1 whole egg and 4 egg whites scrambled; ½ grapefruit
Supplements		Multivitamin	Multivitamin
Meal 2	P/GF	½ cup cottage cheese; ½ grapefruit	1 cup cottage cheese; ½ grapefruit
Meal 3	P/V/O	3–4 oz. chunk tuna on salad with 1 tbsp. extra-virgin olive oil and vinegar	6–8 oz. chunk tuna on salad with 1 tbsp. extra-virgin olive oil and vinegar
Meal 4	P	Chocolate raspberry shake: 20–25 g chocolate protein powder added to 10–12 oz. premade raspberry Crystal Light drink	Chocolate raspberry shake: 30–40 g chocolate protein powder added to 10–12 oz. premade raspberry Crystal Light drink
Meal 5	P/V/V	4 oz. rotisserie chicken; 1 cup broccoli; small house salad with 1 tbsp. extra-virgin olive oil and vinegar	8 oz. rotisserie chicken; 1 cup broccoli; small house salad with 1 tbsp. extra-virgin olive oil and vinegar
Supplements		Multivitamin and antioxidant	Multivitamin and antioxidant
Meal 6	P	Orange dream shake: 20–25 g protein powder added to 10–12 oz. premade orange-pineapple Crystal Light drink	Orange dream shake: 30–40 g protein powder added to 10–12 oz. premade orange-pineapple Crystal Light drink

Notes: For the alternative plan, remove the grapefruit from meal 1 and add veggies to the omelet; remove the grapefruit from meal 2. The rest of the day can remain the same. Do weights first, then cardio. Men who have less than 20 pounds to lose don't need as much cardio. Men who want more muscle definition should do weights 3–5 days per week.

Success Tracker: Week 5—MIC

DAY 29: Monday—Grapefruit (GF)

Affirmation: "I love and care for my body, and it cares for me."

Date: _____

Meals, Drinks, and Snacks

8 oz. water: ○ ○ ○ ○ ○ ○ ○ ○
○ ○ ○ ○ ○ ○ ○ ○

Breakfast: _____   Time: _____

Snack: _____   Time: _____

Lunch: _____   Time: _____

Snack: _____   Time: _____

Dinner: _____   Time: _____

Supplements Taken: _____

_____

_____

Exercise: _____

_____

_____

How do you feel today? _____

_____

_____

Describe your activity level: _____

_____

_____

Did you have any food cravings? How did you manage? _____

_____

_____

Target Plan: Week 5—MIC

DAY 30: Tuesday—Baseline (B)

Carbs: 1 starchy carb at breakfast *and* lunch

ACTION	TYPE	WOMEN	MEN
Meal 1	P/S	1 whole egg and 3 whites scrambled; 2 slices Ezekiel toast	2 whole eggs and 4 whites scrambled; 2 slices Ezekiel toast
Supplements		Multivitamin	Multivitamin
Meal 2	P	Mocha shake: 20–25 g chocolate protein powder added to 8 oz. water in a blender; add 1 heaping tsp. decaf or regular instant coffee and ice for desired thickness.	Mocha shake: 30–40 g chocolate protein powder added to 8 oz. water in a blender; add 1 heaping tsp. decaf or regular instant coffee and ice for desired thickness.
Meal 3	P/S/V	4 oz. tuna on 2 slices Ezekiel bread; small salad	6 oz. tuna on 2 slices Ezekiel bread; salad
Meal 4	P	Vanilla shake: Add 20–25 g vanilla protein powder to 10–12 oz. water in a blender; add ice for desired thickness and blend.	Vanilla shake: Add 30–40 g vanilla protein powder to 10–12 oz. water in a blender; add ice for desired thickness and blend.
Exercise		45–60 minutes EPOC	45–60 minutes EPOC
Supplements		Lipotropic before workout; 1,000 mg vitamin C after workout	Lipotropic before workout; 1,000 mg vitamin C after workout
Meal 5	P/V/V	4 oz. filet mignon; 1 cup sautéed spinach; small house salad with 1 tbsp. extra-virgin olive oil and vinegar	6 oz. filet mignon; 1 cup sautéed spinach; house salad with 1 tbsp. extra-virgin olive oil and vinegar
Supplements		Multivitamin and antioxidant	Multivitamin and antioxidant
Meal 6	P	Crispy lettuce wrap: 2–3 oz. turkey breast and cheese rolled in fresh romaine leaves	Crispy lettuce wrap: 3–5 oz. turkey breast and cheese rolled in fresh romaine leaves

Notes: Not a weight-training day. When you're doing EPOC—in a gym with cardio equipment or outside—keep a consistent pace. Men who have less than 20 pounds to lose don't need as much cardio. Men who want more muscle definition should do weights 3–5 days per week.

Success Tracker: Week 5—MIC

DAY 30: Tuesday—Baseline (B)

Affirmation: "I respect my abilities and always work to my full potential."

Date: _____

Meals, Drinks, and Snacks

8 oz. water: ○ ○ ○ ○ ○ ○ ○ ○
○ ○ ○ ○ ○ ○ ○ ○

Breakfast: _____   Time: _____

Snack: _____   Time: _____

Lunch: _____   Time: _____

Snack: _____   Time: _____

Dinner: _____   Time: _____

Supplements Taken: _____

_____

_____

Exercise: _____

_____

_____

How do you feel today? _____

_____

_____

Describe your activity level: _____

_____

_____

Did you have any food cravings? How did you manage? _____

_____

_____

Target Plan: Week 5—MIC

DAY 31: Wednesday—Grapefruit (GF)

Grapefruit: At first two meals

ACTION	TYPE	WOMEN	MEN
Exercise		Weights (lower body routine); 15–30 minutes HIIT	Weights (lower body routine); 15–30 minutes HIIT
Supplements		L-carnitine or lipotropic before workout; 1,000 mg vitamin C after workout	20 g protein powder mixed in water before workout; 1,000 mg vitamin C after workout
Meal 1	P/GF	½ cup cottage cheese; ½ grapefruit	1 cup cottage cheese; ½ grapefruit
Supplements		Multivitamin	Multivitamin
Meal 2	P/GF	Vanilla shake: 20–25 g vanilla protein powder added to 10–12 oz. water in a blender; add ice for desired thickness and blend. 4 oz. grapefruit juice	Vanilla shake: 30–40 g vanilla protein powder added to 10–12 oz. water in a blender; add ice for desired thickness and blend. 6 oz. grapefruit juice
Meal 3	P/V/O	3–4 oz. grilled chicken on salad with 1 tbsp. extra-virgin olive oil and vinegar	6–8 oz. grilled chicken on salad with 1 tbsp. extra-virgin olive oil and vinegar
Meal 4	P	Mocha shake: 20–25 g chocolate protein powder added to 8 oz. water in a blender; add 1 heaping tsp. decaf or regular instant coffee and ice for desired thickness.	Mocha shake: 30–40 g chocolate protein powder added to 8 oz. water in a blender; add 1 heaping tsp. decaf or regular instant coffee and ice for desired thickness.
Meal 5	P/V/V	6 oz. shrimp and scallop kabobs; grilled eggplant and veggies; small house salad with 1 tbsp. extra-virgin olive oil and vinegar	8 oz. shrimp and scallop kabobs; grilled eggplant and veggies; house salad with 1 tbsp. extra-virgin olive oil and vinegar
Supplements		Multivitamin and antioxidant	Multivitamin and antioxidant
Meal 6	P	Orange dream shake: 20–25 g protein powder added to 10–12 oz. premade orange-pineapple Crystal Light drink	Orange dream shake: 30–40 g protein powder added to 10–12 oz. premade orange-pineapple Crystal Light drink

Notes: For the alternative plan, remove the grapefruit from meals 1 and 2. The rest of the day can remain the same. Do weights first, then cardio. Men who have less than 20 pounds to lose don't need as much cardio. Men who want more muscle definition should do weights 3–5 days per week.

Success Tracker: Week 5—MIC

DAY 31: Wednesday—Grapefruit (GF)

Affirmation: "My inner vision is always clear and focused."

Date: _____

Meals, Drinks, and Snacks

8 oz. water: ○ ○ ○ ○ ○ ○ ○ ○
○ ○ ○ ○ ○ ○ ○ ○

Breakfast: _____ Time: _____

Snack: _____ Time: _____

Lunch: _____ Time: _____

Snack: _____ Time: _____

Dinner: _____ Time: _____

Supplements Taken: _____

_____

_____

Exercise: _____

_____

_____

How do you feel today? _____

_____

_____

Describe your activity level: _____

_____

_____

Did you have any food cravings? How did you manage? _____

_____

_____

Target Plan: Week 5—MIC

DAY 32: Thursday—Baseline (B)

Carbs: 1 starchy carb at breakfast *and* lunch

ACTION	TYPE	WOMEN	MEN
Meal 1	P/S	Wendy's crepe: Mix together 3 egg whites, 1 scoop protein powder, ½ cup oatmeal, and ⅛ cup water for batter. Top with 1 serving sugar-free syrup or sugarless jam.	Wendy's crepe: Mix together 5 egg whites, 2 scoops protein powder, ¾ cup oatmeal, and ⅛ cup water for batter. Top with 1 serving sugar-free syrup or sugarless jam.
Supplements		Multivitamin	Multivitamin
Meal 2	P	Mocha shake: 20–25 g chocolate protein powder added to 8 oz. water in a blender; add 1 heaping tsp. decaf or regular instant coffee and ice for desired thickness.	Mocha shake: 30–40 g chocolate protein powder added to 8 oz. water in a blender; add 1 heaping tsp. decaf or regular instant coffee and ice for desired thickness.
Meal 3	P/S/V	Five-Alarm Chili (See Index.)	Five-Alarm Chili (See Index.)
Meal 4	P	4 oz. shrimp cocktail	6 oz. shrimp cocktail
Meal 5	P/V/V	4–6 oz. roasted turkey breast; 1 cup steamed veggies; small house salad with 1 tbsp. extra-virgin olive oil and vinegar	6–8 oz. roasted turkey breast; 1 cup steamed veggies; house salad with 1 tbsp. extra-virgin olive oil and vinegar
Supplements		Multivitamin and antioxidant	Multivitamin and antioxidant
Meal 6	P	Vanilla shake: Add 20–25 g vanilla protein powder to 10–12 oz. water in a blender; add ice for desired thickness and blend.	Vanilla shake: Add 30–40 g vanilla protein powder to 10–12 oz. water in a blender; add ice for desired thickness and blend.

Notes: Not a weight training day. Recovery is important to the entire body. Rest gives the body a chance to heal and rejuvenate. Don't underestimate the importance of a day off. In good weather I use this time for recreational activities. This is a great time to get the kids involved in fitness too.

Success Tracker: Week 5—MIC

DAY 32: Thursday—Baseline (B)

Affirmation: "I do all I can to follow and stick to my plan."

Date: _____

Meals, Drinks, and Snacks

8 oz. water: ⚪ ⚪ ⚪ ⚪ ⚪ ⚪ ⚪ ⚪
⚪ ⚪ ⚪ ⚪ ⚪ ⚪ ⚪ ⚪

Breakfast: _____   Time: _____

Snack: _____   Time: _____

Lunch: _____   Time: _____

Snack: _____   Time: _____

Dinner: _____   Time: _____

Supplements Taken: _____

_____

_____

Exercise: _____

_____

_____

How do you feel today? _____

_____

_____

Describe your activity level: _____

_____

_____

Did you have any food cravings? How did you manage? _____

_____

_____

Target Plan: Week 5—MIC

DAY 33: Friday—Grapefruit (GF)

Grapefruit: At first two meals

ACTION	TYPE	WOMEN	MEN
Exercise		Weights (shoulders, arms, and abs); 15–30 minutes HIIT	Weights (shoulders, arms, and abs); 15–30 minutes HIIT
Supplements		L-carnitine or lipotropic before workout; 1,000 mg vitamin C after workout	20 g protein powder mixed in water before workout; 1,000 mg vitamin C after workout
Meal 1	P/GF	1 poached egg; ½ grapefruit	2 poached eggs; ½ grapefruit
Supplements		Multivitamin	Multivitamin
Meal 2	P/GF	Vanilla shake: 20–25 g vanilla protein powder added to 10–12 oz. water in a blender; add ice for desired thickness and blend. 4 oz. grapefruit juice	Vanilla shake: 30–40 g vanilla protein powder added to 10–12 oz. water in a blender; add ice for desired thickness and blend. 6 oz. grapefruit juice
Meal 3	P/V/O	Chef salad: 3–4 oz. deli meats and cheese, 1 whole hard-boiled egg, lettuce, and cucumber with 1 tbsp. extra-virgin olive oil and vinegar	Chef salad: 6 oz. deli meats and cheese, 2 whole hard-boiled eggs, lettuce, and cucumber with 1 tbsp. extra-virgin olive oil and vinegar
Meal 4	P	Orange dream shake: 20–25 g protein powder added to 10–12 oz. premade orange-pineapple Crystal Light drink	Orange dream shake: 30–40 g protein powder added to 10–12 oz. premade orange-pineapple Crystal Light drink
Meal 5	P/V/V	6 oz. turkey burger on portobello mushroom cap; 1 cup broccoli; small house salad with 1 tbsp. extra-virgin olive oil and vinegar	8 oz. turkey burger on portobello mushroom cap; 1 cup broccoli; house salad with 1 tbsp. extra-virgin olive oil and vinegar
Supplements		Multivitamin and antioxidant	Multivitamin and antioxidant
Meal 6	P	Chocolate raspberry shake: 20–25 g chocolate protein powder added to 10–12 oz. premade raspberry Crystal Light drink	Chocolate raspberry shake: 30–40 g chocolate protein powder added to 10–12 oz. premade raspberry Crystal Light drink

Notes: For the alternative plan, remove the grapefruit from meals 1 and 2. The rest of the day can remain the same. Do weights first, then cardio. Men who have less than 20 pounds to lose don't need as much cardio. Men who want more muscle definition should do weights 3–5 days per week.

Success Tracker: Week 5—MIC

DAY 33: Friday—Grapefruit (GF)

Affirmation: "I accept my body as it changes, and I feel good."

Date: _____

Meals, Drinks, and Snacks

8 oz. water: ○ ○ ○ ○ ○ ○ ○ ○
○ ○ ○ ○ ○ ○ ○ ○

Breakfast: _____ Time: _____

Snack: _____ Time: _____

Lunch: _____ Time: _____

Snack: _____ Time: _____

Dinner: _____ Time: _____

Supplements Taken: _____

_____

_____

Exercise: _____

_____

_____

How do you feel today? _____

_____

_____

Describe your activity level: _____

_____

_____

Did you have any food cravings? How did you manage? _____

_____

_____

Target Plan: Week 5—MIC

DAY 34: Saturday—Carb Up (D)

Carbs: Last two meals predominantly starchy carbs, including sweets and alcohol

ACTION	TYPE	WOMEN	MEN
Exercise		15–30 minutes HIIT	15–30 minutes HIIT
Supplements		L-carnitine or lipotripic before workout	L-carnitine or lipotripic before workout
Meal 1	P/A	Fake French Toast (See Index.) with side of berries	Fake French Toast (See Index.) with side of berries
Supplements		Multivitamin and 1,000 mg vitamin C	Multivitamin and 1,000 mg vitamin C
Meal 2	P	Yogurt Smoothie (See Index.)	Yogurt Smoothie (See Index.)
Meal 3	P/S	Five-Alarm Chili (See Index.); crackers	Five-Alarm Chili (See Index.); crackers
Meal 4	SA	Popcorn	Popcorn
Supplements		Supplement containing chromium (such as Lean Out)	Supplement containing chromium (such as Lean Out)
Meal 5	SA	Pizza (Don't stuff.); 1 lite beer	Pizza (Don't stuff.); 1 lite beer
Supplements		Multivitamin, antioxidant, and supplement containing chromium (such as Lean Out)	Multivitamin, antioxidant, and supplement containing chromium (such as Lean Out)

Notes: Do your cardio workout first thing in the morning because yesterday was a carb-down day. This morning is the best time to guarantee that your body will use excess fat as an energy source. Do a full 30 minutes. Take a supplement that contains chromium to help keep your blood sugar levels lower, minimizing fat storage. We carry Lean Out at ForeverFit; it is manufactured by Beverly International. Use it to lower blood sugar and promote energy from food.

Success Tracker: Week 5—MIC

DAY 34: Saturday—Carb Up (D)

Affirmation: "I make my own decisions about what to order when eating out."

Date: _____

Meals, Drinks, and Snacks

8 oz. water: ○ ○ ○ ○ ○ ○ ○ ○
    ○ ○ ○ ○ ○ ○ ○ ○

Breakfast: _____   Time: _____

Snack: _____   Time: _____

Lunch: _____   Time: _____

Snack: _____   Time: _____

Dinner: _____   Time: _____

Supplements Taken: _____

_____

_____

Exercise: _____

_____

_____

How do you feel today? _____

_____

_____

Describe your activity level: _____

_____

_____

Did you have any food cravings? How did you manage? _____

_____

_____

Target Plan: Week 5—MIC

DAY 35: Sunday—Baseline (B)

Carbs: 1 starchy carb at breakfast *and* lunch

ACTION	TYPE	WOMEN	MEN
Meal 1	P/S	Protein Oatmeal (See Index.)	Protein Oatmeal (See Index.)
Supplements		Multivitamin	Multivitamin
Meal 2	P	Crispy lettuce wrap: 2–3 oz. turkey breast and cheese rolled in fresh romaine leaves	Crispy lettuce wrap: 3–5 oz. turkey breast and cheese rolled in fresh romaine leaves
Meal 3	P/S	Taco Salad (See Index.); ½ cup rice	Taco Salad (See Index.); 1 cup rice
Meal 4	P	Mocha shake: 20–25 g chocolate protein powder added to 8 oz. water in a blender; add 1 heaping tsp. decaf or regular instant coffee and ice for desired thickness.	Mocha shake: 30–40 g chocolate protein powder added to 8 oz. water in a blender; add 1 heaping tsp. decaf or regular instant coffee and ice for desired thickness.
Exercise		45–60 minutes EPOC	45–60 minutes EPOC
Supplements		Lipotropic before workout; 1,000 mg vitamin C after workout	Lipotropic before workout; 1,000 mg vitamin C after workout
Meal 5	P/V/V	4 oz. rotisserie chicken; 1 cup broccoli; small house salad with 1 tbsp. extra-virgin olive oil and vinegar	8 oz. rotisserie chicken; 1 cup broccoli; house salad with 1 tbsp. extra-virgin olive oil and vinegar
Supplements		Multivitamin and antioxidant	Multivitamin and antioxidant
Meal 6	P	Vanilla shake: Add 20–25 g vanilla protein powder to 10–12 oz. water in a blender; add ice for desired thickness and blend.	Vanilla shake: Add 30–40 g vanilla protein powder to 10–12 oz. water in a blender; add ice for desired thickness and blend.

Notes: Not a weight-training day. When you're doing EPOC—in a gym with cardio equipment or outside—keep a consistent pace. Men who have less than 20 pounds to lose don't need as much cardio. Men who want more muscle definition should do weights 3–5 days per week.

Success Tracker: Week 5—MIC

DAY 35: Sunday—Baseline (B)

Affirmation: "I am free to be myself."

Date: _____

Meals, Drinks, and Snacks

8 oz. water: ○ ○ ○ ○ ○ ○ ○ ○
　　　　　　　　 ○ ○ ○ ○ ○ ○ ○ ○

Breakfast: _____   Time: _____

Snack: _____   Time: _____

Lunch: _____   Time: _____

Snack: _____   Time: _____

Dinner: _____   Time: _____

Supplements Taken: _____

_____

_____

Exercise: _____

_____

_____

How do you feel today? _____

_____

_____

Describe your activity level: _____

_____

_____

Did you have any food cravings? How did you manage? _____

_____

_____

6

Weeks 6–8:
Metabolic Adaptation Cycle
(MAC) Daily Success Planner

The MAC is the first diet cycle ever to overcome every type of adaptive response the body has to stop you from losing weight. To refresh your memory, your body is not designed for fat loss, and as soon as you start manipulating calories by increasing or decreasing food intake, your body responds by doing the very thing you don't want it to do—storing fat. Your body's job is survival, and it does its job by making a series of complicated calculations to balance its energy resources and the performance of its various functions 24/7; for your body to perform these functions, it must adapt.

Think for a moment about your first day on a new job. You jump in and do your best to find ways to make yourself more efficient; to this end, you start putting appropriate systems in place and organizing the way you do things. Your body does the same thing; it uses its adaptive ability to organize and perform its many functions better and more efficiently.

So this cycle takes into account the five ways your body uses adaptation to be efficient. Here is a breakdown of the ways we'll address these five adaptive responses:

1. Manipulate glycogen, which is stored energy derived from glucose formed from carbohydrate consumption. You deplete carbs in this program to force your body to find fat stores when it needs energy. Long-term use of carb depletion actually hinders fat loss because of the overall reduction in hormones and chemicals—such as thyroid output and growth hormone factors—that help your body lose fat.

2. **Manipulate blood sugar levels.** Increased blood sugar levels promote fat storage; balanced levels make your body capable of using stored fatty acids as a source of energy. More fibrous carbohydrates and fewer days of sugary carb consumption will promote more balanced blood sugar levels. Macro-patterning and the MAC plan have some days when you'll need to take in low-glycemic carbs. Many diets today, such as the South Beach Diet, NutriSystem, The Zone, and 40-30-30, use only low-glycemic foods. Such diets are hard to live with over the long term, and most people eventually abandon these types of plans.

3. **Manipulate nitrogen balance and healthy muscle.** Protein is the only macronutrient that maintains and releases nitrogen to keep your muscles healthy. When you don't consume enough protein each day, muscle becomes unhealthy and a negative nitrogen balance is present. Your body sees such muscle as a liability and uses the unhealthy muscle tissue instead of fatty acids as a source of energy. The key is to keep your muscles healthy and have a positive nitrogen balance by consuming protein throughout the day. This is a very important part of macro-patterning and the MAC plan.

4. **Manipulate your calorie intake.** Calorie reduction is one way to force an energy deficit that leads to fatty acids being used as energy. The MAC is the only cycle in which calorie reduction is used (minimally), because your body quickly "senses" calorie reduction. If you follow a reduced-calorie diet continually, your body almost immediately begins to conserve energy and reduce its metabolic rate. The Weight Watcher's points program is an example of a calorie-reduction plan.

5. **Manipulate your body's need for constant and continual energy.** When your body doesn't have an ongoing feeding pattern, it assumes that the last meal you gave it is the last meal it

will get. Your eating pattern determines how and if your body uses the food you take in immediately or whether it stores it for later use. Eating every three to four hours isn't always convenient, but it's one of the major keys to the MAC plan. You also manipulate meal portions to stimulate your metabolic rate, which is called *hypercaloric eating*. When you follow diet or meal plans in which you consume five or six small meals a day, for many months your body gets used to the amount of fuel intake, adapts, and slows your metabolism; this makes many of these diets ineffective. The MAC plan manipulates portion size.

To the dieter, the body becoming more efficient has always meant failing, hitting a plateau, getting stuck, not seeing the needle on the scale move, and giving up. Until now! This revolutionary food plan cycle works best if you follow it for no more than twenty-one days; it is not meant to be used forever. This plan is great to get you "unstuck" from a diet plateau and works especially well if you have dieted a lot through the years. And it really sparks your metabolic rate when you follow it properly.

The MAC is the first and only plan that considers the body's every adaptive means and, best of all, overcomes them. This plan manipulates glycogen stores and includes days when your blood sugar is kept level with the consumption of low-glycemic carbohydrates. You maintain a positive nitrogen balance with proper protein intake and reduce calories to force an energy deficit. Finally, you manipulate portion sizes to force a spike in metabolism.

Conquer the Code

Don't be afraid to try new things. This plan encourages and even demands change, so you might as well accept it. There's never been a better time to start than with the next three weeks!

Metabolic Adaptation Cycle

WEEKS 6 THROUGH 8

	MONDAY DAY 36/43/50	TUESDAY DAY 37/44/51	WEDNESDAY DAY 38/45/52	THURSDAY DAY 39/46/53	FRIDAY DAY 40/47/54	SATURDAY DAY 41/48/55	SUNDAY DAY 42/49/56
Protein Amount	Women, 3–4 oz.; men, 5–6 oz.	Women, 3–4 oz.; men, 5–6 oz.	Women, 3–4 oz.; men, 5–6 oz.	Women, 3–4 oz.; men, 5–6 oz.	Women, 3–4 oz.; men, 5–6 oz.	Cheat	Women, 3–4 oz.; men, 5–6 oz.
Fats	Up	Down	Down	Up	Down	Cheat	Down
Carbs	Zero	Down	Baseline	Zero	Down	Cheat	Baseline

Guidelines for Metabolic Increase Cycle

The MAC guidelines are a bit more complicated than those for the two previous meal cycles. I've given you the basic dos and don'ts, then broken out considerations for specific days.

General Rules

1. Drink eight to ten glasses of water daily.

2. An appropriate serving of protein, such as meat, is usually the size of your palm. For women, this equates to 3 to 4 ounces; for men, it is 5 to 6 ounces

3. You must eat proteins at every meal *except* the following:
   • Protein is not required at all on cheat days.
   • On fats-up days, eat protein at every meal except for "fat snacks."

4. Eat only proteins from MAC food list.

Fats-Up/Carbs-Zero Day

1. Keep portion sizes smaller than you're used to.

2. Eat at least six meals per day.

3. Eat every two to three hours.

4. You may (and should) eat red meat.

5. Eat a fat snack between breakfast and lunch and between lunch and dinner.

6. Limit yourself to 1 cup of vegetables at lunch and dinner.

7. Eat only fats and vegetables from the MAC food list.

8. You may not have salads.

Fats-Down/Carbs-Down Day

1. Keep portion sizes smaller than you're used to.

2. Eat at least six meals per day.

3. Eat every two to three hours.

4. Keep your fat intake to a minimum and avoid all saturated fats.

5. You may have only supplemental fats, such as essential fatty acid supplements or flaxseed oil.

6. Limit yourself to 1 cup of vegetables at lunch and dinner.

7. Do not eat red meat or whole eggs.

8. You may not have salads.

9. Eat only fats and vegetables from the MAC food list.

Fats-Down/Carbs-Baseline Day

1. On Wednesday, eat at least four meals per day; five meals are ideal. Eat every three to four hours, and be sure meals have typical portion sizes.

2. On Sunday, eat at least three meals and consume larger portions (vacation meal size).

3. Eat starchy carbs from the MAC food list.

4. Women may have one serving of starchy carbs at two different meals.

5. Men may have one serving of starchy carbs at three different meals.

6. You may substitute a fruit for a starch at any meal before 3 P.M.

Cheat Day

1. Eat whatever you want in any amount.

2. Use the recommended supplements as directed on these days.

Substitution Food Lists for the Metabolic Adaptation Cycle

The following food substitution list is used for the MAC plan.

Type P = Protein Requirements and Substitutions

1. When eating egg whites, you may have one whole egg with your whites if desired.

2. Eat any of the following proteins.
   a. Egg whites or egg substitute
   b. Chicken breast
   c. Turkey breast

    d. Fresh fish: salmon, trout, and so on

    e. Lean beef

    f. Tuna

    g. Shellfish

    h. ½ cup skim milk

Type S = Starchy Carbohydrates Requirements and Substitutions

1. Consume *only* the following starchy carbs in the specified amounts.

    a. Oatmeal (½ cup dry measure)

    b. Grits (1 serving per package label)

    c. Oat bran (½ cup)

    d. Cream of Rice or Wheat (1 serving per package label)

    e. Cheerios (½ cup)

    f. Rice (½ cup cooked)

    g. Ezekiel bread—flourless bread or millet bread (2 slices)

    h. Beans, any type (½ cup cooked)

    i. Whole-grain pasta (1 cup cooked)

Type V = Vegetable Requirements and Substitutions

1. You may consume 1 cup of any of the following vegetables.

    a. Broccoli

    b. Asparagus

    c. Green beans

    d. Squash

    e. Spinach

    f. Cabbage

    g. Brussels sprouts

    h. Eggplant

Type O = Fat Requirements and Substitutions

1. You may consume any of the following fats.
   a. Almonds or walnuts (10 to 12)
   b. 1 hard-boiled egg
   c. 1 tablespoon oil (any)
   d. Canadian bacon (no more than 2 slices)
   e. Sugar-free low-fat yogurt (4–6 oz.)
   f. 1 mozzarella cheese stick
   g. 1 tablespoon natural peanut butter
   h. 1 percent cottage cheese (4–6 oz.)

Type A = Fruit Requirements and Substitutions

1. You may have one to two servings of any fruit.

Type SA = Sweets and Alcohol Requirements and Substitutions

1. If you have more than 30 pounds to lose, limit sweets and alcohol to help you reach your goal faster.

2. It is recommended that diabetics never consume alcohol.

3. The following are examples of the types of foods you can have for type SA.
   a. Pizza
   b. Pasta
   c. Bagels
   d. Crackers
   e. Breads
   f. French fries
   g. Chips and snacks
   h. Corn, beets, or carrots
   i. Ice cream
   j. Alcohol
   k. Sugary pastries
   l. Cakes

Additional Foods for Fats-Down/Carbs-Baseline Days

1. You may have these foods only on fats-down/carbs-baseline days.
   a. Sugar-free gelatin (limit 2)
   b. No-fat, no-sugar pudding (limit 2)
   c. Small salads eaten with a meal (no fatty dressings; may include tomato, onion, croutons, and cucumber)

Condiments

1. You may use these freely, except where limits are noted.
   a. Salt
   b. Horseradish
   c. Splenda
   d. Pepper (any kind)
   e. Butter Buds®
   f. Vinegar
   g. Ketchup
   h. Garlic
   i. Mustard

Conquer the Code

Make good use of your substitution options. I know it can be tempting to eat the same things day after day, but this is a time when your body is changing, so why not switch your routine as well? If you're tired of broccoli, try a new cauliflower recipe. If you're tired of mocha smoothies, try something with berries. The best part of this life plan is that it actively encourages you to find suitable alternatives throughout the year.

Sample Cardio and Weight Training for the Metabolic Adaptation Cycle

The MAC is a great plan to complement your weight-training and cardio activities. It will supercharge your fat loss and have your body looking *incredible* by the end of the eight weeks! On this plan, you have four great opportunities for weight training because of the greater reduction in carbs and calories. Monday, Tuesday, Thursday, and Friday are days when you will have an energy deficit and are peak times to lose excess fat, especially with about thirty minutes of intense weight training and fifteen to thirty minutes of HIIT cardio. Doing weight training over four days will also allow you to focus on parts of your body where fat holds on stubbornly. Remember that training sessions need to last only about thirty minutes, so we aren't talking about a lot of time in the gym.

There are two ways to handle a four-day training week:

1. Do an upper, lower, upper, lower routine. For instance, focus your first few reps on upper body exercises such as bicep curls or bench presses, and then work on your calves or thighs for a series of reps. Alternate muscle groups this way until your workout is over.

2. Instead of alternating between your upper and lower body, focus on specific body parts by working a big-muscle group followed by a small-muscle group. For example, you could work on your chest (big-muscle group) then triceps (small-muscle group), back (big) then biceps (small), and shoulders and work your legs on a different day.

With either method, doing HIIT after weight training optimizes fat loss. Wednesday and Saturday are also good days for doing cardio first thing in the morning (before breakfast). Sunday works best for a day off with the MAC plan.

DAY	MONDAY	TUESDAY	WENDESDAY	THURSDAY	FRIDAY	SATURDAY	SUNDAY
Type day	Fats up/ carbs zero	Fats down/ carbs down	Fats down/ carbs baseline	Fats up/ carbs zero	Fats down/ carbs down	Cheat	Fats down/ carbs baseline
Weight-training days	Workout	Workout		Workout	Workout		Off
Cardio type	HIIT	HIIT	HIIT	HIIT	HIIT	EPOC	Off
Cardio amount	15–30 minutes	15–30 minutes	30 minutes	15–30 minutes	15–30 minutes	60 minutes	Off
Cardio time of day	1st in morning *or* after workout	1st in morning *or* after workout	1st in morning	1st in morning *or* after workout	1st in morning *or* after workout	1st in morning	Off

Target Plan: Week 6—MAC

DAY 36: Monday—Fats Up/Carbs Zero

ACTION	TYPE	WOMEN	MEN
Exercise		Weights (upper body routine and abs); 15–30 minutes HIIT	Weights (upper body routine and abs); 15–30 minutes HIIT
Supplements		L-carnitine or lipotropic before workout; 1,000 mg vitamin C after workout	20 g protein powder mixed in water before workout; 1,000 mg vitamin C after workout
Meal 1	P/O	1 whole egg and 2 egg whites scrambled; Canadian bacon (limit 2 slices)	1 whole egg and 4 whites scrambled and topped with 2 oz. lean ground beef and a sprinkle of cheese
Supplements		Multivitamin	Multivitamin
Meal 2	P/O	6 oz. cottage cheese (full-fat brand so carbs are reduced)	Vanilla shake: 30–40 g vanilla protein powder added to 10–12 oz. water in a blender; add ice for desired thickness and blend. 12 almonds
Meal 3	P/V	3–4 oz. grilled chicken breast; 1 cup green beans	4–5 oz. grilled chicken breast; 1 cup green beans
Meal 4	O	1 mozzarella cheese stick	1 hard-boiled egg; 1 mozzarella cheese stick
Meal 5	P/V	4 oz. London broil; 1 cup broccoli	6 oz. London broil; 1 cup broccoli
Supplements		Multivitamin and antioxidant	Multivitamin and antioxidant
Meal 6	P	Chocolate shake: Add 20 g chocolate protein powder to 6 oz. low-fat milk and 4 oz. water; blend.	Chocolate shake: Add 30 g chocolate protein powder to 6 oz. low-fat milk and 4 oz. water; blend.

Notes: You may (and should) eat red meat. Eat a fat snack between breakfast and lunch and between lunch and dinner. Limit yourself to 1 cup of vegetables at lunch and dinner. Eat only fats and vegetables from the MAC food list. You may not have salads. Keep portion sizes smaller than you're used to. Eat at least six meals per day.

Success Tracker: Week 6—MAC

DAY 36: Monday—Fats Up/Carbs Zero

Affirmation: "I have provided a harmonious place for myself and those I love."

Date: _____

Meals, Drinks, and Snacks

8 oz. water: ○ ○ ○ ○ ○ ○ ○ ○
○ ○ ○ ○ ○ ○ ○ ○

Breakfast: _____ Time: _____

Snack: _____ Time: _____

Lunch: _____ Time: _____

Snack: _____ Time: _____

Dinner: _____ Time: _____

Supplements Taken: _____

_____

_____

Exercise: _____

_____

_____

How do you feel today? _____

_____

_____

Describe your activity level: _____

_____

_____

Did you have any food cravings? How did you manage? _____

_____

_____

Target Plan: Week 6—MAC

DAY 37: Tuesday—Fats Down/Carbs Down

ACTION	TYPE	WOMEN	MEN
Exercise		Weights (lower body routine and abs); 15-30 minutes HIIT	Weights (lower body routine and abs); 15 minutes HIIT
Supplements		L-carnitine or lipotropic before workout; 1,000 mg vitamin C after workout	20 g protein powder mixed in water before workout; 1,000 mg vitamin C after workout
Meal 1	P/S	3-4 egg whites scrambled; ½ cup oatmeal with 2 packets sugar substitute and cinnamon	4-6 egg whites scrambled; ¾ cup oatmeal with 3 packets sugar substitute and cinnamon
Supplements		Multivitamin	Multivitamin
Meal 2	P	Vanilla shake: Add 20-25 g vanilla protein powder to 10-12 oz. water in a blender; add ice for desired thickness and blend.	Vanilla shake: Add 30-40 g vanilla protein powder to 10-12 oz. water in a blender; add ice for desired thickness and blend.
Meal 3	P/V	3-4 oz. chunk tuna on baby spinach greens	6-8 oz. chunk tuna on baby spinach greens
Meal 4	P	Orange dream shake: 20-25 g protein powder added to 10-12 oz. premade orange-pineapple Crystal Light drink	Orange dream shake: 30-40 g protein powder added to 10-12 oz. premade orange-pineapple Crystal Light drink
Meal 5	P/V	4 oz. cajun grilled chicken; 1 cup steamed veggies	4 oz. cajun grilled chicken; 1 cup steamed veggies
Supplements		Multivitamin and antioxidant	Multivitamin and antioxidant
Meal 6	P	Chocolate raspberry shake: 20-25 g chocolate protein powder added to 10-12 oz. premade raspberry Crystal Light drink	Chocolate raspberry shake: 30-40 g chocolate protein powder added to 10-12 oz. premade raspberry Crystal Light drink

Notes: Keep your fat intake to a minimum; avoid all saturated fats. Do not eat red meat or whole eggs. You may have only supplemental fats, such as essential fatty acid supplements or flaxseed oil. You may not have salads. Keep portion sizes smaller than you're used to.

Success Tracker: Week 6—MAC

DAY 37: Tuesday—Fats Down/Carbs Down

Affirmation: "I choose to make positive, healthy choices for myself."

Date: _____

Meals, Drinks, and Snacks

8 oz. water: ○ ○ ○ ○ ○ ○ ○ ○
○ ○ ○ ○ ○ ○ ○ ○

Breakfast: _____   Time: _____

Snack: _____   Time: _____

Lunch: _____   Time: _____

Snack: _____   Time: _____

Dinner: _____   Time: _____

Supplements Taken: _____

_____

_____

Exercise: _____

_____

_____

How do you feel today? _____

_____

_____

Describe your activity level: _____

_____

_____

Did you have any food cravings? How did you manage? _____

_____

_____

Target Plan: Week 6—MAC

DAY 38: Wednesday—Fats Down/Carbs Baseline

ACTION	TYPE	WOMEN	MEN
Exercise		30 minutes of HIIT cardio	30 minutes of HIIT cardio
Supplements		L-carnitine or lipotropic before workout; 1,000 mg vitamin C after workout	L-carnitine or lipotropic before workout; 1,000 mg vitamin C after workout
Meal 1	P/S	½ cup Cheerios with ½ cup skim milk	¾ cup Cheerios with 1 cup skim milk
Supplements		Multivitamin	Multivitamin
Meal 2	P	Vanilla shake: Add 20–25 g vanilla protein powder to 10–12 oz. water in a blender; add ice for desired thickness and blend.	Vanilla shake: Add 30–40 g vanilla protein powder to 10–12 oz. water in a blender; add ice for desired thickness and blend.
Meal 3	P/S/V	4–6 oz. roasted turkey breast; ½ sweet potato; small house salad with 1 tbsp. of extra-virgin olive oil and vinegar	6–8 oz. roasted turkey breast; 1 sweet potato; small house salad with 1 tbsp. of extra-virgin olive oil and vinegar
Meal 4	P	Mocha shake: 20–25 g chocolate protein powder added to 8 oz. water in a blender; add 1 heaping tsp. decaf or regular instant coffee and ice for desired thickness.	Mocha shake: 30–40 g chocolate protein powder added to 8 oz. water in a blender; add 1 heaping tsp. decaf or regular instant coffee and ice for desired thickness.
Meal 5	P/V/O (women) P/S/V (men)	6 oz. grilled salmon; 1 cup sautéed spinach; dinner salad	8 oz. grilled salmon; ½ cup wild rice; dinner salad
Supplements		Multivitamin and antioxidant	Multivitamin and antioxidant
Meal 6	FF	1 serving sugar-free gelatin with 1 tbsp. Reddi Whip spray cream (not Cool Whip)	1 serving sugar-free gelatin with 1 tbsp. Reddi Whip spray cream (not Cool Whip)

Notes: Women may have 1 serving of starchy carbs at 2 different meals. Men may have 1 serving of starchy carbs at 3 different meals. You may substitute a fruit for a starch at any meal before 3 P.M. Eat at least 4 meals per day; 5 meals are ideal. Be sure meals have typical portion sizes.

Success Tracker: Week 6—MAC

DAY 38: Wednesday—Fats Down/Carbs Baseline

Affirmation: "I am passionate about everything in my life, and everything in my life is good."

Date: _____

Meals, Drinks, and Snacks

8 oz. water: ○ ○ ○ ○ ○ ○ ○ ○
○ ○ ○ ○ ○ ○ ○ ○

Breakfast: _____ Time: _____

Snack: _____ Time: _____

Lunch: _____ Time: _____

Snack: _____ Time: _____

Dinner: _____ Time: _____

Supplements Taken: _____

_____

_____

Exercise: _____

_____

_____

How do you feel today? _____

_____

_____

Describe your activity level: _____

_____

_____

Did you have any food cravings? How did you manage? _____

_____

_____

Target Plan: Week 6—MAC

DAY 39: Thursday—Fats Up/Carbs Zero

ACTION	TYPE	WOMEN	MEN
Exercise		Weights (upper body routine and abs): 15–30 minutes HIIT	Weights (upper body routine and abs): 15–30 minutes HIIT
Supplements		L-carnitine or lipotropic before workout; 1,000 mg vitamin C after workout	20 g protein powder mixed in water before workout; 1,000 mg vitamin C after workout
Meal 1	P/O	1 whole egg with 2 whites scrambled Canadian bacon (limit 2)	1 whole egg with 4 whites scrambled topped with 2 oz. lean ground beef and sprinkle of cheese
Supplements		Multivitamin	Multivitamin
Meal 2	P/O	6 oz. plain yogurt with 10 walnuts	8 oz. plain yogurt with 12 walnuts
Meal 3	P/V	4 oz. meat loaf; 1 cup broccoli	8 oz. meat loaf; 1 cup broccoli
Meal 4	O	Celery stick with 1 tbsp. peanut butter	Protein shake made with 20 g protein powder; 1 tbsp. peanut butter
Meal 5	P/V	4 oz. London broil; 1 cup broccoli	6 oz. London broil; 1 cup broccoli
Supplements		Multivitamin and antioxidant	Multivitamin and antioxidant
Meal 6	P/O	Chocolate shake: Add 20 g chocolate protein powder to 6 oz. low-fat milk and 4 oz. water; blend.	Chocolate shake: Add 30 g chocolate protein powder to 6 oz. low-fat milk and 4 oz. water; blend.

Notes: You may have red meat on this day, and it is preferred. Eat a fat snack between breakfast and lunch and lunch and dinner. Only 1 cup of veggies at lunch and dinner is allowed. No salads. Eat fats and veggies from MAC food list. Portion size small (smaller than you're used to). Eat 6 meals minimum.

Success Tracker: Week 6—MAC

DAY 39: Thursday—Fats Up/Carbs Zero

Affirmation: "Water quenches my thirst and energizes my body."

Date: _____

Meals, Drinks, and Snacks

8 oz. water: ○ ○ ○ ○ ○ ○ ○ ○
○ ○ ○ ○ ○ ○ ○ ○

Breakfast: _____ Time: _____

Snack: _____ Time: _____

Lunch: _____ Time: _____

Snack: _____ Time: _____

Dinner: _____ Time: _____

Supplements Taken: _____
_____
_____

Exercise: _____
_____
_____

How do you feel today? _____
_____
_____

Describe your activity level: _____
_____
_____

Did you have any food cravings? How did you manage? _____
_____
_____

Target Plan: Week 6—MAC

DAY 40: Friday—Fats Down/Carbs Down

ACTION	TYPE	WOMEN	MEN
Exercise		Weights (lower body routine and abs); 15–30 minutes HIIT	Weights (lower body routine and abs); 15 minutes HIIT
Supplements		L-carnitine or lipotropic before workout; 1,000 mg vitamin C after workout	20 g protein powder mixed in water before workout; 1,000 mg vitamin C after workout
Meal 1	P/S	Wendy's crepe: Mix together 3 egg whites, 1 scoop protein powder, ½ cup oatmeal, and ⅛ cup water for batter. Top with 1 serving sugar-free syrup or sugarless jam.	Wendy's crepe: Mix together 5 egg whites, 2 scoops protein powder, ¾ cup oatmeal, and ⅛ cup water for batter. Top with 1 serving sugar-free syrup or sugarless jam.
Supplements		Multivitamin	Multivitamin
Meal 2	P	Vanilla shake: Add 20–25 g vanilla protein powder to 10–12 oz. water in a blender; add ice for desired thickness and blend.	Vanilla shake: Add 30–40 g vanilla protein powder to 10–12 oz. water in a blender; add ice for desired thickness and blend.
Meal 3	P/V	4 oz. tuna-stuffed tomato	6 oz. tuna-stuffed tomato
Meal 4	P	Mocha shake: 20–25 g chocolate protein powder added to 8 oz. water in a blender; add 1 heaping tsp. decaf or regular instant coffee and ice for desired thickness.	Mocha shake: 30–40 g chocolate protein powder added to 8 oz. water in a blender; add 1 heaping tsp. decaf or regular instant coffee and ice for desired thickness.
Meal 5	P/V	4 oz. cajun-grilled chicken; 1 cup asparagus	4 oz. cajun-grilled chicken; 1 cup asparagus
Supplements		Multivitamin and antioxidant	Multivitamin and antioxidant
Meal 6	P	Chocolate raspberry shake: 20–25 g chocolate protein powder added to 10–12 oz. premade raspberry Crystal Light drink	Chocolate raspberry shake: 30–40 g chocolate protein powder added to 10–12 oz. premade raspberry Crystal Light drink

Notes: Keep fat intake to a minimum and avoid all saturated fats. Do not eat red meat or whole eggs. You may have only supplemental fats, such as essential fatty acid supplements or flaxseed oil. No salads. Keep portion sizes smaller than you're used to.

Success Tracker: Week 6—MAC

DAY 40: Friday—Fats Down/Carbs Down

Affirmation: "My possibilities are endless."

Date: _____

Meals, Drinks, and Snacks

8 oz. water: ○ ○ ○ ○ ○ ○ ○ ○
○ ○ ○ ○ ○ ○ ○ ○

Breakfast: _____ Time: _____

Snack: _____ Time: _____

Lunch: _____ Time: _____

Snack: _____ Time: _____

Dinner: _____ Time: _____

Supplements Taken: _____

_____

_____

Exercise: _____

_____

_____

How do you feel today? _____

_____

_____

Describe your activity level: _____

_____

_____

Did you have any food cravings? How did you manage? _____

_____

_____

Target Plan: Week 6—MAC

DAY 41: Saturday—Cheat

ACTION	TYPE	WOMEN	MEN
Exercise		60 minutes EPOC	60 minutes EPOC
Supplements		L-carnitine or lipotropic before workout; 1,000 mg vitamin C after workout	L-carnitine or lipotropic before workout; 1,000 mg vitamin C after workout
Meal 1		½ bagel with cream cheese; small bowl of fruit	1 bagel with cream cheese; bowl of fruit
Supplements		Multivitamin	Multivitamin
Meal 2		Vanilla shake: Add 20–25 g vanilla protein powder to 10–12 oz. water in a blender; add ice for desired thickness and blend.	Vanilla shake: Add 30–40 g vanilla protein powder to 10–12 oz. water in a blender; add ice for desired thickness and blend.
Meal 3		6″ submarine sandwich; snack bag chips	6″ submarine sandwich; snack bag chips
Supplements		Supplement containing chromium (such as Lean Out)	Supplement containing chromium (such as Lean Out)
Meal 4		Cheese pizza; 1 lite beer (Don't stuff.)	Cheese pizza; 1 lite beer (Don't stuff.)
Supplements		Multivitamin, antioxidant, and supplement containing chromium (such as Lean Out)	Multivitamin, antioxidant, and supplement containing chromium (such as Lean Out)
Meal 5		1 serving sugar-free gelatin with 1 tbsp. Reddi Whip spray cream (not Cool Whip)	1 serving sugar-free gelatin with 1 tbsp. Reddi Whip spray cream (not Cool Whip)

Notes: Eat whatever you want in any amount. Use recommended supplements as directed. Don't overdo alcohol or sweets the first week.

Success Tracker: Week 6—MAC

DAY 41: Saturday—Cheat

Affirmation: "I will remain confident and unaffected by negative attitudes around me."

Date: _____

Meals, Drinks, and Snacks

8 oz. water: ◯ ◯ ◯ ◯ ◯ ◯ ◯ ◯
◯ ◯ ◯ ◯ ◯ ◯ ◯ ◯

Breakfast: _____   Time: _____

Snack: _____   Time: _____

Lunch: _____   Time: _____

Snack: _____   Time: _____

Dinner: _____   Time: _____

Supplements Taken: _____
_____
_____

Exercise: _____
_____
_____

How do you feel today? _____
_____
_____

Describe your activity level: _____
_____
_____

Did you have any food cravings? How did you manage? _____
_____
_____

Target Plan: Week 6—MAC

DAY 42: Sunday—Fats Down/Carbs Baseline

ACTION	TYPE	WOMEN	MEN
Meal 1	P/S	½ cup skim milk; bowl of cereal	1 cup skim milk; bowl of cereal
Supplements		Multivitamin	Multivitamin
Meal 2	P/S/V	4 oz. chicken; 1 cup whole-grain pasta salad with tomato, cucumber, 1 tbsp. extra-virgin olive oil, and vinegar (or low-calorie, low-sugar dressing)	8 oz. chicken; 1 cup whole-grain pasta salad with tomato, cucumber, 1 tbsp. extra-virgin olive oil, and vinegar (or low-calorie, low-sugar dressing)
Meal 3	P/V/O (women) P/S/V (men)	6 oz. fresh fish; 1 cup spinach; salad with tomato, cucumber, 1 tbsp. extra-virgin olive oil, and vinegar (or low-calorie, low-sugar dressing)	8 oz. fresh fish; ½ cup wild rice; salad with tomato, cucumber, 1 tbsp. extra-virgin olive oil, and vinegar (or low-calorie, low-sugar dressing)
Meal 4	P	Orange dream shake: 20–25 g protein powder added to 10–12 oz. premade orange-pineapple Crystal Light drink	Orange dream shake: 30–40 g protein powder added to 10–12 oz. premade orange-pineapple Crystal Light drink
Supplements		Multivitamin and antioxidant	Multivitamin and antioxidant

Notes: There is no weight training or cardio today. Women may have one serving of starchy carbs at two different meals. Men may have one serving of starchy carbs at three different meals. You may substitute a fruit for a starch at any meal before 3 P.M. Eat at least 3 meals and consume larger portions (vacation meal size).

Success Tracker: Week 6—MAC

DAY 42: Sunday—Fats Down/Carbs Baseline

Affirmation: "I am worthy of love."

Date: _____

Meals, Drinks, and Snacks

8 oz. water: ○ ○ ○ ○ ○ ○ ○ ○
○ ○ ○ ○ ○ ○ ○ ○

Breakfast: _____   Time: _____

Snack: _____   Time: _____

Lunch: _____   Time: _____

Snack: _____   Time: _____

Dinner: _____   Time: _____

Supplements Taken: _____

_____

_____

Exercise: _____

_____

_____

How do you feel today? _____

_____

_____

Describe your activity level: _____

_____

_____

Did you have any food cravings? How did you manage? _____

_____

_____

Target Plan: Week 7—MAC

DAY 43: Monday—Fats Up/Carbs Zero

ACTION	TYPE	WOMEN	MEN
Exercise		Weights (upper body routine and abs); 15–30 minutes HIIT	Weights (upper body routine and abs); 15 minutes HIIT
Supplements		L-carnitine or lipotropic before workout; 1,000 mg vitamin C after workout	20 g protein powder mixed in water before workout; 1,000 mg vitamin C after workout
Meal 1	P/O	4 oz. yogurt with 1 scoop protein powder	1 whole egg and 4 egg whites scrambled and topped with 2 oz. lean ground beef and a sprinkle of cheese
Supplements		Multivitamin	Multivitamin
Meal 2	P/O	6 oz. cottage cheese (full-fat brand so carbs are reduced)	Vanilla shake: 30–40 g vanilla protein powder added to 10–12 oz. water in a blender; add ice for desired thickness and blend. 12 almonds
Meal 3	P/V	3–4 oz. roasted turkey breast; 1 cup steamed veggies	5–8 oz. roasted turkey breast; 1 cup steamed veggies
Meal 4	O	10 almonds	8 oz. cottage cheese (full-fat brand so carbs are reduced)
Meal 5	P/V	6 oz. broiled salmon; 1 cup sautéed spinach	10 oz. broiled salmon; 1 cup sautéed spinach
Supplements		Multivitamin and antioxidant	Multivitamin and antioxidant
Meal 6	P	Chocolate shake: Add 20 g chocolate protein powder to 6 oz. low-fat milk and 4 oz. water; blend.	Chocolate shake: Add 30 g chocolate protein powder to 6 oz. low-fat milk and 4 oz. water; blend.

Notes: You may (and should) eat red meat. Eat a fat snack between breakfast and lunch and between lunch and dinner. Limit yourself to 1 cup of vegetables at lunch and dinner. Eat only fats and vegetables from the MAC food list. No salads. Keep portion sizes smaller than you're used to. Eat at least 6 meals per day.

Success Tracker: Week 7—MAC

DAY 43: Monday—Fats Up/Carbs Zero

Affirmation: "I feel my possibilities are endless."

Date: _____

Meals, Drinks, and Snacks

8 oz. water: ○ ○ ○ ○ ○ ○ ○ ○
                    ○ ○ ○ ○ ○ ○ ○ ○

Breakfast: _____   Time: _____

Snack: _____   Time: _____

Lunch: _____   Time: _____

Snack: _____   Time: _____

Dinner: _____   Time: _____

Supplements Taken: _____

_____

_____

Exercise: _____

_____

_____

How do you feel today? _____

_____

_____

Describe your activity level: _____

_____

_____

Did you have any food cravings? How did you manage? _____

_____

_____

Target Plan: Week 7—MAC

DAY 44: Tuesday—Fats Down/Carbs Down

ACTION	TYPE	WOMEN	MEN
Exercise		Weights (lower body routine and abs); 15–30 minutes HIIT	Weights (lower body routine and abs); 15 minutes HIIT
Supplements		L-carnitine or lipotropic before workout; 1,000 mg vitamin C after workout	20 g protein powder mixed in water before workout; 1,000 mg vitamin C after workout
Meal 1	P/S	Wendy's crepe: Mix together 3 egg whites, 1 scoop protein powder, ½ cup oatmeal, and ⅛ cup water for batter. Top with 1 serving sugar-free syrup or sugarless jam.	Wendy's crepe: Mix together 5 egg whites, 2 scoops protein powder, ¾ cup oatmeal, and ⅛ cup water for batter. Top with 1 serving sugar-free syrup or sugarless jam.
Supplements		Multivitamin	Multivitamin
Meal 2	P	Orange dream shake: 20–25 g protein powder added to 10–12 oz. premade orange-pineapple Crystal Light drink	Orange dream shake: 30–40 g protein powder added to 10–12 oz. premade orange-pineapple Crystal Light drink
Meal 3	P/V	3–4 oz. chunk tuna on baby spinach greens	6–8 oz. chunk tuna on baby spinach greens
Meal 4	P	Vanilla shake: Add 20–25 g vanilla protein powder to 10–12 oz. water in a blender; add ice for desired thickness and blend.	Vanilla shake: Add 30–40 g vanilla protein powder to 10–12 oz. water in a blender; add ice for desired thickness and blend.
Meal 5	P/V	6 oz. shrimp and scallop kabobs; 1 cup steamed veggies	10 oz. shrimp and scallop kabobs; 1 cup steamed veggies
Supplements		Multivitamin and antioxidant	Multivitamin and antioxidant
Meal 6	P	3–4 egg whites scrambled with mushrooms and spinach	4–5 egg whites scrambled with mushrooms and spinach

Notes: Keep your fat intake to a minimum and avoid all saturated fats. Eat no red meat or whole eggs. You may have only supplemental fats, such as essential fatty acid supplements or flaxseed oil. No salads. Keep portion sizes smaller than you're used to.

Success Tracker: Week 7—MAC

DAY 44: Tuesday Fat Down—Carbs Down

Affirmation: "I choose to feel gratitude daily."

Date: _____

Meals, Drinks, and Snacks

8 oz. water: ○ ○ ○ ○ ○ ○ ○ ○
○ ○ ○ ○ ○ ○ ○ ○

Breakfast: _____   Time: _____

Snack: _____   Time: _____

Lunch: _____   Time: _____

Snack: _____   Time: _____

Dinner: _____   Time: _____

Supplements Taken: _____

_____

_____

Exercise: _____

_____

_____

How do you feel today? _____

_____

_____

Describe your activity level: _____

_____

_____

Did you have any food cravings? How did you manage? _____

_____

_____

Target Plan: Week 7—MAC

DAY 45: Wednesday—Fats Down/Carbs Baseline

ACTION	TYPE	WOMEN	MEN
Exercise		30 minutes HIIT	30 minutes HIIT
Supplements		L-carnitine or lipotropic before workout; 1,000 mg vitamin C after	L-carnitine or lipotropic before workout; 1,000 mg vitamin C after
Meal 1	P/S	½ cup skim milk; ½ cup cereal	1 cup skim milk; ¾ cup cereal
Supplements		Multivitamin	Multivitamin
Meal 2	P	Vanilla shake: Add 20–25 g vanilla protein powder to 10–12 oz. water in a blender; add ice for desired thickness and blend.	Vanilla shake: Add 30–40 g vanilla protein powder to 10–12 oz. water in a blender; add ice for desired thickness and blend.
Meal 3	P/S/V	2 sushi rolls of your choice; ginger salad	2 sushi rolls of your choice; ginger salad
Meal 4	P	Mocha shake: 20–25 g chocolate protein powder added to 8 oz. water in a blender; add 1 heaping tsp. decaf or regular instant coffee and ice for desired thickness.	Mocha shake: 30–40 g chocolate protein powder added to 8 oz. water in a blender; add 1 heaping tsp. decaf or regular instant coffee and ice for desired thickness.
Meal 5	P/V/O (women) P/S/V (men)	6 oz. Citrus Tilapia (See Index.); 1 cup sautéed veggies; dinner salad	10 oz. Citrus Tilapia (See Index.); ½ cup wild rice; dinner salad
Supplements		Multivitamin and antioxidant	Multivitamin and antioxidant
Meal 6	FF	1 serving sugar-free gelatin with 1 tbsp. Reddi Whip spray cream (not Cool Whip)	1 serving sugar-free gelatin with 1 tbsp. Reddi Whip spray cream (not Cool Whip)

Notes: Women may have 1 serving of starchy carbs at 2 different meals. Men may have 1 serving of starchy carbs at 3 different meals. You may substitute a fruit for a starch at any meal before 3 P.M. Eat at least 4 meals per day; 5 meals are ideal. Be sure meals have typical portion sizes.

Success Tracker: Week 7—MAC

DAY 45: Wednesday—Fats Down/Carbs Baseline

Affirmation: "My body is healthy and firm and burns fat fast."

Date: _____

Meals, Drinks, and Snacks

8 oz. water: ○ ○ ○ ○ ○ ○ ○ ○
○ ○ ○ ○ ○ ○ ○ ○

Breakfast: _____ Time: _____

Snack: _____ Time: _____

Lunch: _____ Time: _____

Snack: _____ Time: _____

Dinner: _____ Time: _____

Supplements Taken: _____

_____

_____

Exercise: _____

_____

_____

How do you feel today? _____

_____

_____

Describe your activity level: _____

_____

_____

Did you have any food cravings? How did you manage? _____

_____

_____

Target Plan: Week 7—MAC

DAY 46: Thursday—Fats Up/Carbs Zero

ACTION	TYPE	WOMEN	MEN
Exercise		Weights (upper body routine and abs); 15–30 minutes HIIT	Weights (upper body routine and abs); 15 minutes HIIT
Supplements		L-carnitine or lipotropic before workout; 1,000 mg vitamin C after workout	20 g protein powder mixed in water before workout; 1,000 mg vitamin C after workout
Meal 1	P/O	6 oz. plain yogurt; 10 walnuts	8 oz. plain yogurt; 12 walnuts
Supplements		Multivitamin	Multivitamin
Meal 2	P/O	Shake made with 20 g any flavor protein powder and 1 tbsp. peanut butter	Shake made with 30 g any flavor protein powder and 1 tbsp. peanut butter
Meal 3	P/V	4 oz. cubed beef and mushrooms; 1 cup broccoli	8 oz. cubed beef and mushrooms; 1 cup broccoli
Meal 4	O	6 oz. cottage cheese (full-fat brand so carbs are reduced)	8 oz. cottage cheese (full-fat brand so carbs are reduced)
Meal 5	P/V	Grilled shrimp and veggie kabobs	Grilled shrimp and veggie kabobs
Supplements		Multivitamin and antioxidant	Multivitamin and antioxidant
Meal 6	P/O	Chocolate shake: Add 20 g chocolate protein powder to 6 oz. low-fat milk and 4 oz. water; blend.	Chocolate shake: Add 30 g chocolate protein powder to 6 oz. low-fat milk and 4 oz. water; blend.

Notes: You may (and should) eat red meat. Eat a fat snack between breakfast and lunch and between lunch and dinner. Limit yourself to 1 cup of vegetables at lunch and dinner. Eat only fats and vegetables from the MAC food list. No salads. Keep portion sizes smaller than you're used to. Eat at least 6 meals per day.

Success Tracker: Week 7—MAC

DAY 46: Thursday—Fats Up/Carbs Zero

Affirmation: "I have provided a harmonious place for myself and those I love."

Date: _____

Meals, Drinks, and Snacks

8 oz. water: ○ ○ ○ ○ ○ ○ ○ ○
　　　　　　　　 ○ ○ ○ ○ ○ ○ ○ ○

Breakfast: _____   Time: _____

Snack: _____   Time: _____

Lunch: _____   Time: _____

Snack: _____   Time: _____

Dinner: _____   Time: _____

Supplements Taken: _____
_____
_____

Exercise: _____
_____
_____

How do you feel today? _____
_____
_____

Describe your activity level: _____
_____
_____

Did you have any food cravings? How did you manage? _____
_____
_____

Target Plan: Week 7—MAC

DAY 47: Friday—Fats Down/Carbs Down

ACTION	TYPE	WOMEN	MEN
Exercise		Weights (lower body routine and abs); 15–30 minutes HIIT	Weights (lower body routine and abs); 15 minutes HIIT
Supplements		L-carnitine or lipotropic before workout; 1,000 mg vitamin C after workout	20 g potein powder mixed in water before workout; 1,000 mg vitamin C after workout
Meal 1	P/S	Protein Oatmeal (See Index.)	Protein Oatmeal (See Index.)
Supplements		Multivitamin	Multivitamin
Meal 2	P/V	2–3 oz. turkey breast, avocado slices, and cabbage rolled in fresh romaine leaves	3–4 oz. turkey breast, avocado slices, and cabbage rolled in fresh romaine leaves
Meal 3	P/V	Chicken and vegetable soup	Chicken and vegetable soup
Meal 4	P	Mocha shake: 20–25 g chocolate protein powder added to 8 oz. water in a blender; add 1 heaping tsp. decaf or regular instant coffee and ice for desired thickness.	Mocha shake: 30–40 g chocolate protein powder added to 8 oz. water in a blender; add 1 heaping tsp. decaf or regular instant coffee and ice for desired thickness.
Meal 5	P/V	4 oz. baked chicken with crushed tomatoes and basil; 1 cup spaghetti squash	8 oz. baked chicken with crushed tomatoes and basil; 1 cup spaghetti squash
Supplements		Multivitamin and antioxidant	Multivitamin and antioxidant
Meal 6	P	Orange dream shake: 20–25 g protein powder added to 10–12 oz. premade orange-pineapple Crystal Light drink	Orange dream shake: 30–40 g protein powder added to 10–12 oz. premade orange-pineapple Crystal Light drink

Notes: Keep your fat intake to a minimum and avoid all saturated fats. Do not eat red meat or whole eggs. You may have only supplemental fats, such as essential fatty acid supplements or flaxseed oil. No salads. Keep portion sizes smaller than you're used to.

Success Tracker: Week 7—MAC

DAY 47: Friday—Fats Down/Carbs Down

Affirmation: "I'm going to live a long and healthy life."

Date: _____

Meals, Drinks, and Snacks

8 oz. water: ○ ○ ○ ○ ○ ○ ○ ○
                   ○ ○ ○ ○ ○ ○ ○ ○

Breakfast: _____   Time: _____

Snack: _____   Time: _____

Lunch: _____   Time: _____

Snack: _____   Time: _____

Dinner: _____   Time: _____

Supplements Taken: _____

_____

_____

Exercise: _____

_____

_____

How do you feel today? _____

_____

_____

Describe your activity level: _____

_____

_____

Did you have any food cravings? How did you manage? _____

_____

_____

Target Plan: Week 7—MAC

DAY 48: Saturday—Cheat

ACTION	TYPE	WOMEN	MEN
Exercise		60 minutes EPCO	60 minutes EPOC
Supplements		L-carnitine or lipotropic before workout; 1,000 mg vitamin C after workout	L-carnitine or lipotropic before workout; 1,000 mg vitamin C after workout
Meal 1		Breakfast at Cracker Barrel (have anything on the menu)	Breakfast at Cracker Barrel (have anything on the menu)
Supplements		Multivitamin	Multivitamin
Meal 2		Vanilla shake: Add 20–25 g vanilla protein powder to 10–12 oz. water in a blender; add ice for desired thickness and blend.	Vanilla shake: Add 30–40 g vanilla protein powder to 10–12 oz. water in a blender; add ice for desired thickness and blend.
Meal 3		Lunch at Chili's with a friend (have a burger and fries)	Lunch at Chili's with a friend (have a burger and fries)
Supplements		Supplement containing chromium (such as Lean Out)	Supplement containing chromium (such as Lean Out)
Meal 4		Lasagna; roll; 1 glass wine (Don't stuff.)	Lasagna; roll; 1 glass wine (Don't stuff.)
Supplements		Multivitamin, antioxidant, and supplement containing chromium (such as Lean Out)	Multivitamin, antioxidant, and supplement containing chromium (such as Lean Out)
Meal 5		1 serving sugar-free gelatin with 1 tbsp. Reddi Whip spray cream (not Cool Whip)	1 serving sugar-free gelatin with 1 tbsp. Reddi Whip spray cream (not Cool Whip)

Notes: Eat whatever you want in any amount. Use recommended supplements as directed. Don't overdo alcohol or sweets.

Success Tracker: Week 7—MAC

DAY 48: Saturday—Cheat

Affirmation: "Planning my meals guarantees my success."

Date: _____

Meals, Drinks, and Snacks

8 oz. water: ⭕ ⭕ ⭕ ⭕ ⭕ ⭕ ⭕ ⭕
               ⭕ ⭕ ⭕ ⭕ ⭕ ⭕ ⭕ ⭕

Breakfast: _____ Time: _____

Snack: _____ Time: _____

Lunch: _____ Time: _____

Snack: _____ Time: _____

Dinner: _____ Time: _____

Supplements Taken: _____
_____
_____

Exercise: _____
_____
_____

How do you feel today? _____
_____
_____

Describe your activity level: _____
_____
_____

Did you have any food cravings? How did you manage? _____
_____
_____

Target Plan: Week 7—MAC

DAY 49: Sunday—Fats Down/Carbs Baseline

ACTION	TYPE	WOMEN	MEN
Meal 1	P/S	3–4 egg whites scrambled; ¼ cantaloupe	5 egg whites scrambled; ¼ cantaloupe
Supplements		Multivitamin	Multivitamin
Meal 2	P/S/V	4 oz. tuna fish sandwich on 2 slices of favorite bread; side salad	6 oz. tuna fish sandwich on 2 slices of favorite bread; side salad
Meal 3	P/V/O (women) P/S/V (men)	6 oz. roasted turkey; 1cup green beans; salad with tomatoes, cucumber, 1 tbsp. extra-virgin olive oil, and vinegar (or low-calorie, low-sugar dressing)	8 oz. roasted turkey; 1 sweet potato; salad with tomatoes, cucumber, 1 tbsp. extra-virgin olive oil, and vinegar (or low-calorie, low-sugar dressing)
Meal 4	P	Vanilla shake: Add 20–25 g vanilla protein powder to 10–12 oz. water in a blender; add ice for desired thickness and blend.	Vanilla shake: Add 30–40 g vanilla protein powder to 10–12 oz. water in a blender; add ice for desired thickness and blend.
Supplements		Multivitamin and antioxidant	Multivitamin and antioxidant

Notes: No weight training or cardio today. Women may have 1 serving of starchy carbs at 2 different meals. Men may have 1 serving of starchy carbs at 3 different meals. You may substitute a fruit for a starch at any meal before 3 P.M. Eat at least 3 meals and consume larger portions (vacation meal size).

Success Tracker: Week 7—MAC

DAY 49: Sunday—Fats Down/Carbs Baseline

Affirmation: "I have a healthy heart and lungs and a strong immune system."

Date: _____

Meals, Drinks, and Snacks

8 oz. water: ○ ○ ○ ○ ○ ○ ○ ○
○ ○ ○ ○ ○ ○ ○ ○

Breakfast: _____ Time: _____

Snack: _____ Time: _____

Lunch: _____ Time: _____

Snack: _____ Time: _____

Dinner: _____ Time: _____

Supplements Taken: _____

_____

_____

Exercise: _____

_____

_____

How do you feel today? _____

_____

_____

Describe your activity level: _____

_____

_____

Did you have any food cravings? How did you manage? _____

_____

_____

Target Plan: Week 8—MAC

DAY 50: Monday—Fats Up/Carbs Zero

ACTION	TYPE	WOMEN	MEN
Exercise		Weights (upper body routine and abs); 15–30 minutes HIIT	Weights (upper body routine and abs); 15 minutes HIIT
Supplements		L-carnitine or lipotropic before workout; 1,000 mg vitamin C after workout	20 g protein powder mixed in water before workout; 1,000 mg vitamin C after workout
Meal 1	P/O	1 whole egg and 2 egg whites scrambled; Canadian bacon (limit 2 slices)	1 whole egg and 4 egg whites scrambled and topped with 2 oz. lean ground beef and a sprinkle of cheese
Supplements		Multivitamin	Multivitamin
Meal 2	P/O	6 oz. cottage cheese (full-fat brand so carbs are reduced)	Vanilla shake: Add 30–40 g vanilla protein powder to 10–12 oz. water in a blender; add ice for desired thickness and blend. 12 almonds
Meal 3	P/V	3–4 oz. turkey breast; 1 cup green beans	4–5 oz. turkey breast; 1 cup green beans
Meal 4	O	1 mozzarella cheese stick	1 whole hard-boiled egg; 1 mozzarella cheese stick
Meal 5	P/V	4 oz. filet mignon; 1 cup broccoli	6 oz. filet mignon; 1 cup broccoli
Supplements		Multivitamin and antioxidant	Multivitamin and antioxidant
Meal 6	P	Chocolate shake: Add 20 g chocolate protein powder to 6 oz. low-fat milk and 4 oz. water; blend.	Chocolate shake: Add 30 g chocolate protein powder to 6 oz. low-fat milk and 4 oz. water; blend.

Notes: You may (and should) eat red meat. Eat a fat snack between breakfast and lunch and between lunch and dinner. Limit yourself to 1 cup of vegetables at lunch and dinner. Eat only fats and vegetables from the MAC food list. No salads. Keep portion sizes smaller than you're used to. Eat at least 6 meals per day.

Success Tracker: Week 8—MAC

DAY 50: Monday—Fats Up/Carbs Zero

Affirmation: "I am powerful at pursuing my dreams."

Date: _____

Meals, Drinks, and Snacks

8 oz. water: ○ ○ ○ ○ ○ ○ ○ ○
○ ○ ○ ○ ○ ○ ○ ○

Breakfast: _____   Time: _____

Snack: _____   Time: _____

Lunch: _____   Time: _____

Snack: _____   Time: _____

Dinner: _____   Time: _____

Supplements Taken: _____

_____

_____

Exercise: _____

_____

_____

How do you feel today? _____

_____

_____

Describe your activity level: _____

_____

_____

Did you have any food cravings? How did you manage? _____

_____

_____

Target Plan: Week 8—MAC

DAY 51: Tuesday—Fats Down/Carbs Down

ACTION	TYPE	WOMEN	MEN
Exercise		Weights (lower body routine and abs); 15–30 minutes HIIT	Weights (lower body routine and abs); 15 minutes HIIT
Supplements		L-carnitine or lipotropic before workout; 1,000 mg vitamin C after workout	20 g protein powder mixed in water before workout; 1,000 mg vitamin C after workout
Meal 1	P/S	Wendy's crepe: Mix together 3 egg whites, 1 scoop protein powder, ½ cup oatmeal, and ⅛ cup water for batter. Top with 1 serving sugar-free syrup or sugarless jam.	Wendy's crepe: Mix together 5 egg whites, 2 scoops protein powder, ¾ cup oatmeal, and ⅛ cup water for batter. Top with 1 serving sugar-free syrup or sugarless jam.
Supplements		Multivitamin	Multivitamin
Meal 2	P	Vanilla shake: Add 20–25 g vanilla protein powder to 10–12 oz. water in a blender; add ice for desired thickness and blend.	Vanilla shake: Add 30–40 g vanilla protein powder to 10–12 oz. water in a blender; add ice for desired thickness and blend.
Meal 3	P/V	Turkey burger on portobello mushroom cap	Turkey burger on portobello mushroom cap
Meal 4	P	Orange dream shake: 20–25 g protein powder added to 10–12 oz. premade orange-pineapple Crystal Light drink	Orange dream shake: 30–40 g protein powder added to 10–12 oz. premade orange-pineapple Crystal Light drink
Meal 5	P/V	6 oz. grilled halibut; 1 cup steamed veggies	8 oz. grilled halibut; 1 cup steamed veggies
Supplements		Multivitamin and antioxidant	Multivitamin and antioxidant
Meal 6	P	Chocolate raspberry shake: 20–25 g chocolate protein powder added to 10–12 oz. premade raspberry Crystal Light drink	Chocolate raspberry shake: 30–40 g chocolate protein powder added to 10–12 oz. premade raspberry Crystal Light drink

Notes: Keep your fat intake to a minimum and avoid all saturated fats. Do not eat red meat or whole eggs. You may have only supplemental fats, such as essential fatty acid supplements or flaxseed oil. No salads. Keep portion sizes smaller than you're used to.

Success Tracker: Week 8—MAC

DAY 51: Tuesday—Fats Down/Carbs Down

Affirmation: "I focus on my meal plan, and my meals are all delicious."

Date: _____

Meals, Drinks, and Snacks

8 oz. water: ○ ○ ○ ○ ○ ○ ○ ○
              ○ ○ ○ ○ ○ ○ ○ ○

Breakfast: _____   Time: _____

Snack: _____   Time: _____

Lunch: _____   Time: _____

Snack: _____   Time: _____

Dinner: _____   Time: _____

Supplements Taken: _____

_____

_____

Exercise: _____

_____

_____

How do you feel today? _____

_____

_____

Describe your activity level: _____

_____

_____

Did you have any food cravings? How did you manage? _____

_____

_____

Target Plan: Week 8—MAC

DAY 52: Wednesday—Fats Down/Carbs Baseline

ACTION	TYPE	WOMEN	MEN
Exercise		30 minutes HIIT	30 minutes HIIT
Supplements		L-carnitine or lipotropic before workout; 1,000 mg vitamin C after	L-carnitine or lipotropic before workout; 1,000 mg vitamin C after
Meal 1	P/S/A	Protein Oatmeal (See Index) with bananas	Protein Oatmeal (See Index) with bananas
Supplements		Multivitamin	Multivitamin
Meal 2	P	Vanilla shake: Add 20–25 g vanilla protein powder to 10–12 oz. water in a blender; add ice for desired thickness and blend.	Vanilla shake: Add 30–40 g vanilla protein powder to 10–12 oz. water in a blender; add ice for desired thickness and blend.
Meal 3	P/S/V	4–6 oz. roasted turkey breast; ½ sweet potato; small house salad with 1 tbsp. extra-virgin olive oil and vinegar	6–8 oz. roasted turkey breast; 1 sweet potato; house salad with 1 tbsp. extra-virgin olive oil and vinegar
Meal 4	P	Mocha shake: 20–25 g chocolate protein powder added to 8 oz. water in a blender; add 1 heaping tsp. decaf or regular instant coffee and ice for desired thickness.	Mocha shake: 30–40 g chocolate protein powder added to 8 oz. water in a blender; add 1 heaping tsp. decaf or regular instant coffee and ice for desired thickness.
Meal 5	P/V/O (women) P/S/V (men)	6 oz. grilled lobster; 1 cup sautéed spinach; dinner salad	8 oz. grilled lobster; 1 baked potato; dinner salad
Supplements		Multivitamin and antioxidant	Multivitamin and antioxidant
Meal 6	FF	1 serving sugar-free gelatin with 1 tbsp. Reddi Whip spray cream (not Cool Whip)	1 serving sugar-free gelatin with 1 tbsp. Reddi Whip spray cream (not Cool Whip)

Notes: Women may have 1 serving of starchy carbs at 2 different meals. Men may have 1 serving of starchy carbs at 3 different meals. You may substitute a fruit for a starch at any meal before 3 P.M. Eat at least 4 meals per day; 5 meals are ideal. Be sure meals have typical portion sizes.

Success Tracker: Week 8—MAC

DAY 52: Wednesday—Fats Down/Carbs Baseline

Affirmation: "My body is a fat-burning machine."

Date: _____

Meals, Drinks, and Snacks

8 oz. water: ○ ○ ○ ○ ○ ○ ○ ○
○ ○ ○ ○ ○ ○ ○ ○

Breakfast: _____ Time: _____

Snack: _____ Time: _____

Lunch: _____ Time: _____

Snack: _____ Time: _____

Dinner: _____ Time: _____

Supplements Taken: _____

_____

_____

Exercise: _____

_____

_____

How do you feel today? _____

_____

_____

Describe your activity level: _____

_____

_____

Did you have any food cravings? How did you manage? _____

_____

_____

Target Plan: Week 8—MAC

DAY 53: Thursday—Fats Up/Carbs Zero

ACTION	TYPE	WOMEN	MEN
Exercise		Weights (upper body routine and abs); 15–30 minutes HIIT	Weights (upper body routine and abs); 15 minutes HIIT
Supplements		L-carnitine or lipotropic before workout; 1,000 mg vitamin C after workout	20 g protein powder mixed in water before workout; 1,000 mg vitamin C after workout
Meal 1	P/O	1 whole egg and 2 egg whites scrambled; Canadian bacon (limit 2 slices)	1 whole egg and 4 whites scrambled and topped with 2 oz. lean ground beef and a sprinkle of cheese
Supplements		Multivitamin	Multivitamin
Meal 2	P/O	6 oz. plain yogurt; 10 walnuts	8 oz. plain yogurt; 12 walnuts
Meal 3	P/V	4 oz. meat loaf; 1 cup broccoli	8 oz. meat loaf; 1 cup broccoli
Meal 4	O	Shake made with 20 g any flavor protein powder and 1 tbsp. peanut butter	Shake made with 30 g any flavor protein powder and 1 tbsp. peanut butter
Meal 5	P/V	Smoked beef ribs; grilled veggies	Smoked beef ribs; grilled veggies
Supplements		Multivitamin and antioxidant	Multivitamin and antioxidant
Meal 6	P/O	Chocolate shake: Add 20 g chocolate protein powder to 6 oz. low-fat milk and 4 oz. water; blend.	Chocolate shake: Add 30 g chocolate protein powder to 6 oz. low-fat milk and 4 oz. water; blend.

Notes: You may (and should) eat red meat. Eat a fat snack between breakfast and lunch and between lunch and dinner. Limit yourself to 1 cup of vegetables at lunch and dinner. Eat only fats and vegetables from the MAC food list. No salads. Keep portion sizes smaller than you're used to. Eat at least 6 meals per day.

Success Tracker: Week 8—MAC

DAY 53: Thursday—Fats Up/Carbs Zero

Affirmation: "Every day when I wake up, my body feels thinner and firmer."

Date: _____

Meals, Drinks, and Snacks

8 oz. water: ○ ○ ○ ○ ○ ○ ○ ○
○ ○ ○ ○ ○ ○ ○ ○

Breakfast: _____   Time: _____

Snack: _____   Time: _____

Lunch: _____   Time: _____

Snack: _____   Time: _____

Dinner: _____   Time: _____

Supplements Taken: _____

_____

_____

Exercise: _____

_____

_____

How do you feel today? _____

_____

_____

Describe your activity level: _____

_____

_____

Did you have any food cravings? How did you manage? _____

_____

_____

Target Plan: Week 8—MAC

DAY 54: Friday—Fats Down/Carbs Down

ACTION	TYPE	WOMEN	MEN
Exercise		Weights (lower body routine and abs); 15–30 minutes HIIT	Weights (lower body routine and abs); 15 minutes HIIT
Supplements		L-carnitine or lipotropic before workout; 1,000 mg vitamin C after workout	20 g protein powder mixed in water before workout; 1,000 mg vitamin C after workout
Meal 1	P/S	Wendy's crepe: Mix together 3 egg whites, 1 scoop protein powder, ½ cup oatmeal, and ⅛ cup water for batter. Top with 1 serving sugar-free syrup or sugarless jam.	Wendy's crepe: Mix together 5 egg whites, 2 scoops protein powder, ¾ cup oatmeal, and ⅛ cup water for batter. Top with 1 serving sugar-free syrup or sugarless jam.
Supplements		Multivitamin	Multivitamin
Meal 2	P	Vanilla shake: Add 20–25 g vanilla protein powder to 10–12 oz. water in a blender; add ice for desired thickness and blend.	Vanilla shake: Add 30–40 g vanilla protein powder to 10–12 oz. water in a blender; add ice for desired thickness and blend.
Meal 3	P/V	Tomato stuffed with 4 oz. tuna	Tomato stuffed with 6 oz. tuna
Meal 4	P	Mocha shake: 20–25 g chocolate protein powder added to 8 oz. water in a blender; add 1 heaping tsp. decaf or regular instant coffee and ice for desired thickness.	Mocha shake: 30–40 g chocolate protein powder added to 8 oz. water in a blender; add 1 heaping tsp. decaf or regular instant coffee and ice for desired thickness.
Meal 5	P/V	4 oz. cajun-grilled chicken; 1 cup asparagus	4 oz. cajun-grilled chicken; 1 cup asparagus
Supplements		Multivitamin and antioxidant	Multivitamin and antioxidant
Meal 6	P	Chocolate raspberry shake: 20–25 g chocolate protein powder added to 10–12 oz. premade raspberry Crystal Light drink	Chocolate raspberry shake: 30–40 g chocolate protein powder added to 10–12 oz. premade raspberry Crystal Light drink

Notes: Keep your fat intake to a minimum and avoid all saturated fats. Do not eat red meat or whole eggs. You may have only supplemental fats, such as essential fatty acid supplements or flaxseed oil. No salads. Keep portion sizes smaller than you're used to.

Success Tracker: Week 8—MAC

DAY 54: Friday—Fats Down/Carbs Down

Affirmation: "Losing fat has become easy for me."

Date: _____

Meals, Drinks, and Snacks

8 oz. water: ○ ○ ○ ○ ○ ○ ○ ○
             ○ ○ ○ ○ ○ ○ ○ ○

Breakfast: _____   Time: _____

Snack: _____   Time: _____

Lunch: _____   Time: _____

Snack: _____   Time: _____

Dinner: _____   Time: _____

Supplements Taken: _____

_____

_____

Exercise: _____

_____

_____

How do you feel today? _____

_____

_____

Describe your activity level: _____

_____

_____

Did you have any food cravings? How did you manage? _____

_____

_____

Target Plan: Week 8—MAC

DAY 55: Saturday—Cheat

ACTION	TYPE	WOMEN	MEN
Exercise		60 minutes EPOC	60 minutes EPOC
Supplements		L-carnitine or lipotropic before workout; 1,000 mg vitamin C after workout	L-carnitine or lipotropic before workout; 1,000 mg vitamin C after workout
Meal 1		½ bagel with cream cheese; small bowl of fruit	1 bagel with cream cheese; bowl of fruit
Supplements		Multivitamin	Multivitamin
Meal 2		Vanilla shake: Add 20–25 g vanilla protein powder to 10–12 oz. water in a blender; add ice for desired thickness and blend.	Vanilla shake: Add 30–40 g vanilla protein powder to 10–12 oz. water in a blender; add ice for desired thickness and blend.
Meal 3		6″ submarine sandwich; snack bag chips	6″ submarine sandwich; snack bag chips
Supplements		Supplement containing chromium (such as Lean Out)	Supplement containing chromium (such as Lean Out)
Meal 4		Cheese pizza; 1 lite beer (Don't stuff.)	Cheese pizza; 1 lite beer (Don't stuff.)
Supplements		Multivitamin, antioxidant, and supplement containing chromium (such as Lean Out)	Multivitamin, antioxidant, and supplement containing chromium (such as Lean Out)
Meal 5		1 serving sugar-free gelatin with 1 tbsp. Reddi Whip spray cream (not Cool Whip)	1 serving sugar-free gelatin with 1 tbsp. Reddi Whip spray cream (not Cool Whip)

Notes: Eat whatever you want in any amount. Use recommended supplements as directed. Don't overdo alcohol or sweets.

Success Tracker: Week 8—MAC

DAY 55: Saturday—Cheat

Affirmation: "I look in the mirror, and I see a beautiful, thin, and vibrant person."

Date: _____

Meals, Drinks, and Snacks

8 oz. water: ○ ○ ○ ○ ○ ○ ○ ○
○ ○ ○ ○ ○ ○ ○ ○

Breakfast: _____   Time: _____

Snack: _____   Time: _____

Lunch: _____   Time: _____

Snack: _____   Time: _____

Dinner: _____   Time: _____

Supplements Taken: _____

_____

_____

Exercise: _____

_____

_____

How do you feel today? _____

_____

_____

Describe your activity level: _____

_____

_____

Did you have any food cravings? How did you manage? _____

_____

_____

Target Plan: Week 8—MAC

DAY 56 SUNDAY—FATS DOWN/CARBS BASELINE

ACTION	TYPE	WOMEN	MEN
Meal 1	P/S	½ cup skim milk; bowl cereal	1 cup skim milk; bowl cereal
Supplements		Multivitamin	Multivitamin
Meal 2	P/S/V	4 oz. chicken; 1 cup whole-grain pasta salad with tomatoes, cucumber, 1 tbsp. extra-virgin olive oil, and vinegar (or low-calorie, low-sugar dressing)	8 oz. chicken; 1 cup whole-grain pasta salad with tomatoes, cucumber, 1 tbsp. extra-virgin olive oil, and vinegar (or low-calorie, low-sugar dressing)
Meal 3	P/V/O (women) P/S/V (men)	6 oz. fresh fish; 1 cup spinach; salad with tomatoes, cucumber, 1 tbsp. extra-virgin olive oil, and vinegar (or low-calorie, low-sugar dressing)	8 oz. fresh fish; ½ cup wild rice; salad with tomatoes, cucumber, 1 tbsp. extra-virgin olive oil, and vinegar (or low-calorie, low-sugar dressing)
Meal 4	P	Orange dream shake: 20–25 g protein powder added to 10–12 oz. premade orange-pineapple Crystal Light drink	Orange dream shake: 30–40 g protein powder added to 10–12 oz. premade orange-pineapple Crystal Light drink
Supplements		Multivitamin and antioxidant	Multivitamin and antioxidant

Notes: No weight training or cardio today. Women may have 1 serving of starchy carbs at 2 different meals. Men may have 1 serving of starchy carbs at 3 different meals. You may substitute a fruit for a starch at any meal before 3 P.M. Eat at least 3 meals and consume larger portions (vacation meal size).

Success Tracker: Week 8—MAC

DAY 56 SUNDAY—FATS DOWN/CARBS BASELINE

Affirmation: "I support healthy living as it has supported me."

Date: _____

Meals, Drinks, and Snacks

8 oz. water: ○ ○ ○ ○ ○ ○ ○ ○
　　　　　　　 ○ ○ ○ ○ ○ ○ ○ ○

Breakfast: _____   Time: _____

Snack: _____   Time: _____

Lunch: _____   Time: _____

Snack: _____   Time: _____

Dinner: _____   Time: _____

Supplements Taken: _____

_____

_____

Exercise: _____

_____

_____

How do you feel today? _____

_____

_____

Describe your activity level: _____

_____

_____

Did you have any food cravings? How did you manage? _____

_____

_____

PART 3

Tips, Tactics, and Tools for Success

7

Flexible Planning for Weekends, Traveling, Holidays, and Time Off

I have had more success on this program with *no guilt*, *more food*, and *complete flexibility* in my meal plans. . . . I love it, and I would recommend it to anyone who has stalled and is frustrated on that "diet plateau"!

—*Alissa V. Maxwell, proud code cracker*

Several things can sabotage fat-loss plans—weekends, travel, holidays, and even simple time off. It seems the minute the weather turns cold, the trick-or-treat ghosts and goblins walk the streets, or the clock strikes five on Friday afternoon, those carefully structured meal plans go right out the window.

Well, guess what—you can't give up weekends, holidays, or time off. In fact, you shouldn't want to! They are necessary for your mental health, and for better or worse, food, drink, and indulgence are a big part of them. You can make it better when you simply look at eating right and moving more as long-range goals that allow for the occasional extravagance and fantastic buffet.

The idea is not to deny yourself; the idea is to recognize both cracking and conquering the fat-loss code as lifestyle plans in which pleasure, fun, and life in general are built in.

Weekends: Don't Let These Forty-Eight Hours Become a Mystery

Ah, the weekend! Time to kick off your shoes, get comfy, and overindulge, right? Well, maybe not. Weekends have been sabotaging diets for as long as there have been diets, but it's not typically the actual food you eat that derails your plan so quickly or effectively. It's how you *feel* about the food you eat that does the most damage.

Think of all the hard work you did during the week: exercising before work, taking your lunch to work, steaming your vegetables, boiling brown rice, grilling your chicken. Then, bam! It's the weekend, and your first stop is a fast-food drive-through on the way home, or you order some pizza, soda, buffalo wings, and dessert to go with your Friday night fright fest.

You're tired on Saturday, so you don't work out, and with that extra hour or two to kill, you feel hungry and head out to the doughnut shop or pancake house. Since the day is already blown by noon, you keep going and eat whatever you want, for as long as you want, sleep in on Sunday, and start the same routine all over again.

Come Monday, you're feeling down and blue but determined to get back on track. Of course, if you'd just played it cool over the weekend, you'd be cruising along with plenty of positive momentum instead of starting from a sitting position.

The worst part is that if you had a healthier, more cheat-friendly attitude going into the weekend, you likely wouldn't have gone as far off the rails in the first place. Remember: a missed workout here and an extra slice of pizza there aren't even cheating when you're conquering the fat-loss code, but we've been trained by so many so-called diet experts for so long to feel guilty about these little treats that once we indulge, there is nothing left to do but overindulge.

Want some advice? Good, because here it is: give yourself a break! Enjoy the weekend, sleep in, work out a little later, eat a little more, and stay up longer, but don't go so completely off the rails that you blow your plan altogether. Stay loose but keep things in check, and just think about how great you'll feel Monday morning when you don't have to start from scratch.

I have clients who absolutely know that every weekend they're going to eat their high-carb comfort foods. This is just the way it is for them. So to prevent wasting the beginning of every week playing catch-up, we simply plan ahead. By following the "book-end" philosophy, we make sure they follow two back-to-back carb-down or deplete days on Thursday and Friday.

Deplete Day (A)

Deplete is a serious word for serious business, but that's exactly what we're going to be doing in the first week of your program. I call it your "seven-day diet." This is the only time I really use the word *diet* to refer to my program, and I use it in the strictest sense. This is when you're restricting certain foods—particularly carbs—and manipulating the amount of glycogen that is stored in your muscles. During deplete days, you are going to shut off your body's dependence on sugar and teach it where fat stores are available for its energy needs.

Remember to put your carb-up and cheat days back-to-back on Saturday and Sunday and then follow with Monday and Tuesday as carb-down and deplete days.

Sample Plan for Weekend Indulgence

MONDAY	TUESDAY	WEDNESDAY	THURSDAY	FRIDAY	SATURDAY	SUNDAY
Deplete	Carb down	Baseline	Carb down	Deplete	Carb up	Cheat

By planning ahead for weekend indulgences, you never feel guilty, because your weekend is officially part of your unique program. Remember, it's not about filling in charts and graphs and staying locked into a dull routine. This program is designed with interchangeable parts for a realistic, hectic, and human lifestyle.

Traveling

If I had a nickel for every time I heard how a long weekend, two-week vacation, or quick business trip derailed somebody's fat-loss plan, I'd be rich. Traveling can lead us to break from our daily routine, which is a great way for the mind to tempt us with new restaurants, new dishes, and new reasons for sabotaging any success we might have had back home.

While dieting is never easy, cooking your own food from your own fridge in your own home gives you much more control over how much you eat and when. Eating at home makes sticking to a lifelong plan less complicated and more successful. Shopping at your local grocery store with a set list of approved foods and working out at your neighborhood gym also make things easier because, again, you're in control.

It's that lack of control that makes traveling such a sticky wicket when it comes to staying with your plan. You're busy; you're rushed; you're in a strange place and in a hurry with other people milling around, and you feel pressured to do, have, and eat what everyone else is doing, having, and eating. Not to worry; the tips in this section will help you stick with your plan regardless of what city—or country—you're in.

Plan Ahead to Stay Ahead

No matter where you go or for how long, it's a safe bet you're going to find the same eateries—or types of eateries—along the way. If you don't see the "golden arches," you can "make a run for the border" and "have it your way" somewhere "finger lickin' good" where taste goes "beyond the bun." Get familiar with the best choices at each of the main fast-food chains before you head out of town, so making healthy choices on the go won't put your program in jeopardy.

For instance, nowadays nearly every fast-food chain lists its menu items online, in printable format, so you can clearly see calorie counts, fat grams, and even sodium and protein content in black and white. Many companies even have a special category for their "healthy," "healthful," or "healthier" foods. This means you can always have nutritional information from Burger King, Taco Bell, Panera, McDonald's, Wendy's, and dozens of others available on your laptop or in your carry-on for quick, easy, healthier choices. Highlight your favorite three items in different colors, so you'll always have a few options.

If you want a sit-down meal, you're still covered, because even fancier chain restaurants like Applebee's, Longhorn, Olive Garden, and TGI Friday's post their menus online. Again, you can print them out and choose ahead. Even if you leave your briefcase and your inhibitions back in the hotel room, you're still in luck, because most restaurants list their healthy choices right there on the menu, such as Applebee's Weight Watcher's menu and TGI Friday's Lighter Side menu options.

Flexible Meal Plan for Traveling

Now, even if you don't want to print fast-food menus or look for heart-healthy items in a dark corner booth at your favorite restaurant, a little common sense can help you conquer the fat-loss code no matter where you eat or how long you're away from home.

The first step to fat-loss success while traveling is *not* to leave your plan behind! Both *Crack the Fat-Loss Code* and *Conquer the Fat-Loss Code* were designed to be portable, realistic, and livable. Your fat-loss plan doesn't have to be rigid and static when it comes to the days of the week.

When you understand the true concept of macro-patterning and how it works to affect fat loss in your body, you can then treat your meal plans like a deck of cards; sometimes that means moving a few carb-up days together—like you might on vacation or over an eat-as-you-go business trip—and other times shifting your carb-down or deplete days around to accommodate your plans.

For instance, let's say you're going to a family reunion at Aunt Fannie's and you just know you're not going to get away without sampling a table full of her high-carb goodies. Well, if the trip is from Thursday to Saturday, you can safely bet that you'll be using all your carb-up days for the week while you're away. To plan for the trip without tossing your fat-loss program out the window, you could shift your carb-down days for the week to Monday, Tuesday, and Wednesday. That way your body can still absorb the increase in carbohydrates you'll consume while you're out of town. When you get back, you can shuffle your days around some more and plan to spend Sunday and Monday either carbing down or carb depleting. With these adjustments, you've still had a full week on the plan; you've merely shifted days around to absorb the trip you knew you were going to take two weeks in advance.

Sample Plan for Traveling

MONDAY	TUESDAY	WEDNESDAY	THURSDAY	FRIDAY	SATURDAY	SUNDAY
Advance Plan for Reunion			Family Reunion			Home
Deplete	Deplete	Deplete	Carb up	Cheat	Cheat	Deplete
Deplete	Carb down	Carb up	Baseline	Carb down	Carb up	Baseline

Macro-patterning is all about combining the days of the week for maximum effect, so use your days wisely. When you know you're going to be using several of one type of day in a row, redistribute the other days to compensate. The best part of these meal plans and interchangeable food days is that I've built cheating, vacations, holidays, weekends, and time off into the program. Remember, it's not a diet; it's a lifestyle!

Don't Let Convenience Crash Your Program

There is no reason you should fear or avoid traveling just because you're committed to losing fat. Making fat loss a lifestyle choice means living the program every day; the key word is *living*! That often includes the joy, the surprises, and the excitement of travel.

Eight Quick Trip Tips for Eating When You're on the Road

Planning ahead will make traveling much more enjoyable and less risky when it comes to your fat-loss success and long-range goals. One thing I love to do, even if I'm just in for a long day of traveling to classes here in Central Florida, is to pack a small cooler with the foods on my meal plan. With the wide variety of sizes and styles of thermal packing materials these days, it's easier than ever to put your protein powder in a container and add water later. It's also simple to prepare healthy snacks like turkey and cheese roll-ups; bag veggies or fruit; and even pre-package your salad, dressing, and toppings separately.

Of course, when traveling, you won't always have the "luxury" of eating at a sit-down restaurant or even zipping past a fast-food drive-up window. Sometimes you just have to settle for a quick trip to that highway exit convenience store or gas station.

What do you do when everything on the menu is either bottled, canned, wrapped, nuked, fried, frosted, coated, smothered, or vacuum sealed? Not to fret, my fellow code crackers. Here are eight safe convenience-store picks that won't trash your fat-loss plan:

1. Just because it comes in a bag doesn't mean it can't fit on your substitution list. Pretzels are baked, never fried, and always low fat.

2. Dairy products are a common convenience-store item and, when chosen carefully, make for a quick, healthy

choice. Try yogurt, a small bottle of milk, or single cheese sticks, if available.

3. It's really amazing to see how far some of today's most popular convenience stores have come. It's the rare shop that doesn't have some kind of fresh fruit, so choosing an apple, banana, orange, or other seasonal fruit is now easier than ever.

4. Raisins or other dried fruits can seem like a healthy alternative—and are often labeled as such—but they are also extremely high in sugar. Instead, reach for one of those prepackaged cereal bowls or, if you can't find those, the snack-size boxes of Cheerios or corn flakes.

5. Nuts, in moderation, are always a good choice; try them without the fancy seasonings like "spicy hot," "honey roast," or "chipotle rub."

6. A V-8 or other vegetable juice—or fruit juice—makes a better choice than some flavored coffee shake or sugary soda.

7. Not all teas are created equal. Some are full of sugar, flavorings, preservatives, and other sweeteners, so stick with either diet versions or, preferably, unsweetened or lightly sweetened.

8. Bottled or canned coffee drinks can be loaded with sugar and other flavorings. Try a vitamin water or low-sugar Gatorade instead.

The ForeverFit Holiday Weight-Loss Plan: Cheat, Eat, and Lose Weight

The following holiday plan is designed to allow you to eat whatever you want on any holiday of the year. Trick-or-treat candy on Halloween, as well as the day before and the day after? Go for it! A forty-eight-hour New Year's Eve and New Year's Day extravaganza? Absolutely. I devised this simple solution nearly a decade ago, and my clients now swear by it.

It's basically the same "deck of cards" game I showed you in the section on traveling. You know the holiday is coming well in advance, so use the week before to begin "reshuffling" your carb-down or deplete days. Then enjoy yourself for one, two, or three days, and be sure to follow the holiday with another week of reshuffling meal plans to compensate and get you back on track. Here's how.

Conquer the Code

The trick to losing fat while traveling is to plan ahead. Make a few practice runs while you're still in town so that ordering healthy in fast-food places, sit-down restaurants, and even convenience stores is old hat by the time you hit the road.

Adjust Meal Plan Days for Flexible Holiday Eating

As I mentioned earlier, think of your fat-loss days like bookends. When you know a holiday is coming up, plan to restrict yourself a little more before you indulge and to slowly rein yourself back in after it's over. Between those bookends, the sky's the limit! The best part of following this plan is that you never have to worry about that miserable feeling most people get after the holidays when they've overindulged and have no way to compensate for it. Using my plan, you don't fall off the wagon altogether; you just have to arrange your days in advance to make room for the expected indulgence.

Here's an example of how you can readjust for a holiday like Thanksgiving without gaining any fat. Most people experience a weight loss of two pounds or more when they follow this plan *exactly*.

- **Thursday, November 20: carb-down day.** One starch with protein meals before 3 P.M.

- **Friday, November 21: carb-down day.** One starch with protein meals before 3 P.M.

- **Saturday, November 22: baseline day.** Two starches with protein meals before 3 P.M.

- **Sunday, November 23: baseline day.** Two starches with protein meals before 3 P.M.

- **Monday, November 24–Wednesday, November 26: deplete days** (no starches) **or carb-down days** (one starch with protein meals before 3 P.M.). You choose which type of cycle day based on how much you want to cheat on Thanksgiving. If you are new to the boot camp way of life, I suggest making all three deplete days.

- **Friday, November 27 (Thanksgiving Day): cheat day!** Once you get up, begin eating to keep your metabolism going and allow you to eat enough food. The plan works best if you have small amounts of food every few hours until your big meal, then *overeat* (yes, that's what I said). This will force your body to replenish and replace hormones and chemicals that begin to decline when the body recognizes that dieting is taking place and signals the body to kick your metabolism into high gear to deal with the extra energy the body now has available. This extra spark in metabolism created by the overeat will ultimately help you lose weight.

- **Friday, November 28: deplete day.** This day is the most important part of the holiday plan. *Deplete*! You must make this a deplete day. I suggest doing cardio activity first thing in the morning—for an hour, if you can. If you know that you cannot deplete today, then don't overeat on Thanksgiving. Otherwise, you will not lose the weight.

- **Saturday, November 29: baseline day.** Two starches with protein meals before 3 P.M. or no starches until your last meal of the day, when you have whatever you want. If you are new to the boot camp way of life, I suggest the first option.

- **Sunday, November 30.** Back to whatever plan you are on.

> **Conquer the Code**
> Remember that the day after your cheat day you need to follow a deplete meal plan and perform cardio activity first thing in the morning for an hour.

Time Off: Game On

My program is all about building good habits for a lifetime of healthy living—that's what being forever fit is. After your first eight weeks of conquering the code, the habits of eating better and moving more are more automatic. This makes time off a treat instead of a temptation.

So far we've been doing damage control over the holidays and on weekends, but in this section, I want you to try to take a healthier attitude about your free time. See it as an opportunity rather than a time for failure or "cheating" on your program. The following three suggestions can help you do that.

Do Something Different

Try something new. After all, that's what time off is for! Seriously, the meal plans and exercise introduced in *Conquer the Fat-Loss Code* are just guidelines. There are plenty of alternative and substitution lists that let you add some spice to your life. My target plans are never meant to be strict or inflexible, exact eating plans you had to follow at specific times. So if you've got time off and want to spend it productively, work up some new combinations and put some variety into your routine. Take an extra half hour in the grocery store to discover new vegetables to use in cooking or a new spice to add to your recipes, or simply watch a healthy cooking demonstration. When you've got some extra time, why not grill instead of broil, simmer instead of sear, and make eating an event as opposed to a duty.

Take Your Time

It can be challenging and even unpleasant to cram a forty-five-minute workout into a thirty-minute break or what should be a nice, leisurely meal into less than twenty minutes because you have to rush back to the office. When we're on the go, we find ourselves so busy with things to do that we often feel like we're in a pressure cooker ourselves. When you finally have some breathing room, take the time and enjoy trying new recipes, going on a long walk, or simply stopping by the gym at a different time of day—and staying longer. Reward yourself by doing something fun and leisurely after your workout, like stopping by the farmer's market, sitting in the park with a fresh postgym smoothie, or simply going to the mall and buying something fabulous to show off your new shape. You've got the time; the best way to use it is effectively.

Eat Someplace Special

Time off is an opportunity to break out of the routine and try something new; you should apply that philosophy to how you eat and move. For instance, if you've been sticking closely to your meal plan and want some variation, try a new restaurant and order a meal that goes along with the program but that you didn't have to fix. Salmon cooked at home probably tastes very different from salmon cooked at an upscale restaurant; it may be prepared quite differently from the way you normally cook it.

> **Conquer the Code**
>
> Variety isn't just the spice of life; it's an absolute necessity. When you have holidays, weekends, and time off to enjoy, do so by trying new things and discovering creative, novel ways of preparing food or exercising.

What Do You Do if You Fall Off the Wagon?

In my first book, I introduced the concept that both the body and human nature fight to keep fat on. The minute you start a diet, your body responds by wanting to put more weight back on; it hates to be deprived.

It's the old cookie jar conundrum. Tell a kid to keep his hands out of the cookie jar and what's the first thing he wants to do? Grab a cookie. He may not be hungry, may not even like cookies, but the minute he hears the word *don't*, that's the first thing he wants to do.

The body reacts in the same way. By restricting calories, skipping meals, or otherwise going hungry, you immediately tell your body "don't gain weight." So what's the first thing it wants to do? That's right—gain weight.

That's why I developed the concept of macro-patterning to trick the body into not feeling so deprived and instantly sending signals to your brain to pack on the pounds. But while it may be comparatively easy to distract your body with a little sleight of hand, your brain is another thing altogether.

You and I both know how hard it is to unlearn years, maybe even decades, of intensely ingrained eating habits. How we ate as kids affected how we ate in school, how we ate in school affected how we ate on the weekends, how we ate on the weekends affected how we ate in college, . . . The pattern continues to this very day, so it's understandable if you fall off the wagon every now and then. The trick is to know what to do when that happens.

Two Ways to Handle a Setback

It's only natural for you to succumb to temptation now and again. In fact, that's why I built cheating into my program and make it a prominent player in *Conquer the Fat-Loss Code*. But what happens when you cheat more than once or twice a week? What do you do when you fall off the wagon for a few days or, as happens occasionally, a few weeks?

Well, one of two things can happen:

- You can forgive yourself and get right back on the program.
- You can give up.

Which one do you think I suggest? That's right, get back on that horse. Life is not a race, and fat loss shouldn't have to be either. In fact, you have all the time in the world to lose fat, move more, feel better, and live forever fit.

Having realistic goals is the key to achieving them. The surest way to fall short of your goal is to give yourself an unreasonable time line, expect to lose an unrealistic amount of weight, or pledge to run a marathon "next month" when you've never run farther than the length of a parking lot in your life.

We often concentrate on the physical aspect of fat loss: protein, fat, and carbohydrates; aerobic versus anaerobic forms of exercise; and so on. *Conquer the Fat-Loss Code* also addresses how important and challenging the mental aspect of changing your body type can be. Focus on the positive; be realistic about what you can do. I'd much rather see you reach lots and lots of small, realistic goals that make you feel good about yourself than one dramatic goal that makes headlines. The fact is, the fastest way to fall off the wagon is to give yourself unrealistic deadlines for crossing the finish line.

Use the Three Fs to Soften the Blow

To avoid kicking yourself when you're down and feeling bad about a lapse in your program, I've designed my three Fs to help you get back on track as painlessly and effectively as possible:

- **Forgive.** The first step to getting back on the program is to forgive yourself. You are not "bad," "stupid," "fat," or "lazy" for cheating or even giving up halfway through. Fat loss is an optional decision; you don't *have* to do anything in this world. But if losing fat and moving more *is* important to you and you *do* want to crack the fat-loss code all over again, the first thing you'll have to do is get rid of the negative baggage that's holding you back.

- **Forget.** Act like it never happened; start over with a clean slate. Even if you're halfway through, a third of the way through, or just beginning the program, act like you never fell off the wagon in the first place. When you play a video game and you're just not feeling it, your score isn't as high as you think it should be, or your thumbs are stiff, you can push one button and start all over. Consider this step your official "restart" button!

- **Forge ahead.** Lastly, get back on that horse. The only way to really let falling off the wagon derail you permanently is to stay down on the ground wallowing in your mistakes. Get up, dust off your meal planners, go shopping, take a walk around the block, listen to some energizing music, or just get some fresh air and move on. The sooner you get back on your plan, the sooner you'll get positive effects that will really make you feel successful.

What the Code Crackers Are Saying

Darlean Yankovich

As a child, I was always the little skinny one in the family; I couldn't seem to gain weight, and my parents thought there was something wrong with me. All that changed in my twenties after a bout with depression and my discovery of comfort food, my favorite being potato chips.

By the time I turned forty-eight, I was watching the number on the scale go up weekly, although I was living on salads. I had pretty much resigned myself to the fact that I would be overweight for the rest of my life. Then I saw a friend of mine and noticed she'd lost weight. She told me about Wendy's plan. I was skeptical but decided to give it a try. I also decided it would be my final attempt at losing weight—it hurt too much to constantly fail at dieting.

I started Wendy's food plan, and she explained how and why those diets had failed me rather than the other way around (I'd never even considered that possibility!) and why I had gained weight eating only salads. Then she told me how I could turn all that around.

Well, that was fifty-eight pounds ago! Now at forty-nine, I weigh less than I did when I graduated from high school, and I'm in the best shape of my life. I've also lost more than 26 percent body fat by following Wendy's plan and incorporating her exercise techniques into my lifestyle. Now my body fat is less than 13 percent and I have Wendy and her food and exercise plans to thank.

I have no fear that I'll ever gain that weight back. I now understand how to have my "cheat" meals, enjoy my food and my life, and not add pounds on. I don't have to deprive myself of anything, including my favorite comfort foods. Even holidays are a breeze now, given Wendy's holiday plans. I used to dread them because I would always gain weight, but no more. This plan is not a diet at all; it's my lifestyle and it's second nature to me now.

This is an amazing plan that has totally transformed my life and how I live. I have so much more confidence and self-esteem (not to mention energy!), and that carries over to all areas of my life. I know there are no limits to what I can accomplish in any aspect of my life now. Wendy and her food and exercise plans gave me back my life—and it's better than ever. For that, I am forever grateful!!

8

Quick Tips for Ultimate Success

You bought this book because you wanted to jump-start the successful program you learned in *Crack the Fat-Loss Code*. Well, I wrote this book to introduce you to more concepts and share these quick tips, tactics, and strategies for ultimate success. I've been using them with my clients for years, and now I want to share them with you.

Tips to Boost Your Metabolism

I think you'll really enjoy these simple, easy tips to rev up your metabolism. Not only can you incorporate them into your daily life, but they will accelerate your fat loss even more.

Boost Your Metabolism by What and How You Eat

• **Eat every three to four hours while you're awake.** By eating at regular intervals, you keep your metabolic rate in high gear. Every time you eat, there's a corresponding rise in core body temperature that burns off calories, so eating small, frequent meals triggers several metabolism-revving spikes throughout the day. In fact, according to researchers from the University of Western Australia, using this strategy burns just as many calories in one day as a thirty-minute workout.

• **Make the first meal of the day a "chewing meal."** Don't have a protein shake or smoothie for breakfast. When you sleep at night, your body essentially fasts, and your metabolism slows down, so making the first dish of the day a protein-packed meal that you have to chew stimulates your metabolism and starts the fire burning for the day.

• **Use oatmeal as one of your main starches.** The high fiber count keeps you full longer, and your body rarely wants to store this type of food as fat.

• **Surprise your body with "hypercaloric" meals.** Your body eventually gets used to any kind of routine, even an eating routine, and this causes your metabolism to get sluggish. So if you tend to eat about the same number of calories every day and at every meal, you're headed for a certain diet plateau.

A great and fun way to overcome this inevitability is to plan an overeat meal (or meals). This is called *hypercaloric eating* in the scientific community and is used in such sports as bodybuilding when you're trying to jolt your metabolism to get that last little bit of fat off.

I have my clients use it, especially around holidays like Thanksgiving, where you eat small, low-calorie meals for several days and then start eating everything you can on Turkey Day. Many find it amazing that they actually lose weight over the holiday instead of going back to work with an extra five pounds packed on.

This theory works a lot like the fire you start in a fireplace: as you add more logs, the fire starts burning hotter and faster, and the more logs you add, the faster they are consumed. The same goes for your metabolism; once it is sparked with so much food, your body must "heat up" to deal with all this extra fuel to burn. Your metabolism continues to burn at this hotter rate even days later, so you benefit from a fantastic food-filled holiday and less fat around your middle when you go back to work. If that isn't a win-win situation, I don't know what is.

- **Eat more fat.** Healthy fats like the omega-3 fatty acids found in tuna, salmon, and flaxseed and the monounsaturated fatty acids found in olive oil, nuts, and nut butters have been shown to boost metabolism. In fact, metabolism is significantly higher for five hours after a meal that contains just one serving of these healthy fats. And ditch the skim dairy products and fat-free dressing. Some fat is needed at every meal to boost the absorption of fat-soluble, energy-revving vitamins like vitamin D. Instead, opt for low-fat or full-fat dairy and dressings.

- **Take a daily multivitamin.** It contains nutrients like vitamin B_{12} and magnesium that help keep metabolism-regulating organs like your adrenals and thyroid in full working order. If you still think you need an extra energy and metabolic boost, try taking an additional B_{12} or magnesium supplement.

- **Drink authentic green tea or use a green tea extract.** Green tea can increase core temperature by 4 percent, which can result in up to six to eight pounds lost monthly without a change of diet.

- **Enjoy warming fall and winter spices.** Cinnamon, nutmeg, and cloves, which are used in many cold-weather favorites like pumpkin and apple pie and hot chocolate, are all thermogenic. This means they raise your body's metabolism (sometimes by as much as 78 percent), so you effortlessly burn more calories even when you're resting. As little as half a teaspoon daily gives you the full thermogenic benefit.

- **Eat quality protein to burn more calories.** Did you know that protein can literally heat up your metabolism? That's right. Protein has a high TEF, or thermic effect of food. This TEF is equal to 0.25 times the total number of protein calories ingested, whereas carbohydrates and fat have TEFs that are only 0.04 to 0.06 times the total calories ingested.

In other words, you can count on burning up to five times as many calories when you eat protein as when you eat the other two macronutrients. For every 500 calories of protein you take in, you expend 125 calories through its TEF. Both carbohydrates and fat burn only a measly 30 calories per 500 calories eaten.

• **Avoid artificial sweeteners as much as you can.** Researchers from Purdue University found that the artificial sweeteners in diet sodas and diet foods don't cause a rise in core body temperature as foods normally do. So people who consume them regularly actually end up with a drop in metabolism that sabotages weight-loss goals.

• **Steer clear of stimulants.** There's no doubt that stimulants like nicotine or large amounts of caffeine from energy drinks perk you up at the beginning. But they do it in a way that you have to pay for later, with a big energy slump and slower metabolism.

• **Drink lots of good old water.** It's well known that making sure the body is well hydrated is key to optimal metabolic function. In fact, some studies show about a 33 percent increase in metabolism every time you enjoy a glass of H_2O. Truth is, the standard eight glasses of water (about 64 ounces) doesn't work for everyone. Hydration research gives the following formula for calculating your body's specific needs: divide your weight in pounds by two. So a 150-pound woman should be drinking 75 ounces, which is more like nine to ten glasses a day. Then an additional glass should be consumed for every eight-ounce cup of coffee or other highly caffeinated drink you consume. That's how you're really going to get the metabolism-boosting benefit of water.

Boost Your Metabolism by How You Move

• **Do cardio first thing in the morning on an empty stomach.** You will get more fat loss out of exercise at this time because your glycogen stores are at their lowest.

• **Change your environment occasionally.** One of the ways to force your metabolism into high gear is to adjust the thermogenic effect of environment (TEE), or drastically change the temperature of your current environment. For instance, use a sauna just after exercising to bring your core temperature up, and then take a cool shower after the sauna to push your body to raise its metabolic rate to counteract the change in temperature.

• **Use yoga, meditation, or breathing exercises to counteract stress.** These easy forms of stress relief slash your levels of cortisol, which is a hormone that slows metabolism and causes the storage of excess belly fat. The result of these exercises is an energy boost that enhances your body's ability to burn calories. Try this: breathe in deeply and slowly for a count of five, then exhale slowly for a count of five. Do this for at least one minute several times a day.

• **Get "the wiggles" every hour.** Scientists have found that simply doing some activity at least once every hour prevents metabolism slowdowns and keeps blood sugar stable, warding off weight gain. It can be any kind of activity, even something as simple as walking to a colleague's desk to drop off some forms, standing to organize files or books, taking the long way to the restroom, or rapidly tapping your feet on the floor football-drill style for thirty seconds.

Conquer the Code

Be on the lookout for more tips like this and add them to your personal collection of super-duper secret metabolism boosters! Join trusted, medically endorsed, online weight-loss message boards; host a weekly diet-book club; or simply network with friends to share the best metabolism-boosting tips around.

Staying Motivated with a Fitness Buddy

From time to time, running those lonely miles or making the long, silent trek to the gym can be more than just painful; it can be a real pain in the butt! It's hard to stay motivated doing the same things week in and week out with no one there to cheer you on; pump you up; or just remind you that it's 8 A.M. and time to get your butt out of bed and go for your morning walk, jog, or sprint. Two heads really are better than one, particularly when it comes to moving more and feeling better. I recommend working out with a buddy—or two—whenever possible. Why? Let me count the ways:

- A workout buddy can help keep you motivated by being positive when you're negative and vice versa. Helping others always helps us help ourselves.
- A workout buddy can keep you exercising more regularly with wake-up calls or affirmations throughout the day and week.
- A workout buddy makes working out more fun.
- A workout buddy can remind you that working out isn't just about your body but can often improve your mind and relationships along the way.
- A workout buddy provides support, motivation, and even comic relief.
- Best of all, a workout buddy knows what you're going through and is always there to pick you up, keep you going, and of course cheer you on!

Conquer the Code

Make sure your workout buddy is compatible with your personality and your workout schedule. You want someone who brings you up, not someone who drags you down.

What the Code Crackers Are Saying

Janne Ackerman

I started the program because I had regained thirty pounds and was looking at going into a pair of size 18 pants. No way, no how! About that time I saw an ad in the paper for Wendy's "boot camp" here in Central Florida. I went, I listened to her, and afterward I said, "Pizza and dessert are OK? This is the way for me to go."

The first week on the program I lost seven pounds, and I was eating more food each day than I would have consumed in two or three days without the program. It took very little time to get myself into a routine for setting up my meals and little time to prepare them. Within ten weeks I had dropped to a size 10, closer to a size 8. I had lost inches off my waist, hips, thighs, and butt—even my upper arms looked thinner!

People were constantly telling me that I looked younger because I even lost weight in my face. I had tons more energy, and I was so much more confident and healthy looking. I am a golf operations manager and feel I should promote a healthy, fit persona as a member of the sports community. Thanks to Wendy, now I can!

PART 4

Wendy's "Mmm Good" Recipes

9

Making Wendy's "Mmm Good" Recipes Work for You

I've never considered myself a world-class chef or, for that matter, a real whiz in the kitchen, but apparently some of you do. The response to my "Mmm Good" recipes in *Crack the Fat-Loss Code* was overwhelming. I can't tell you how many voice mails, letters, and e-mails I got raving over this or that recipe. So this time around, I thought I'd put some of that enthusiasm to work!

This section contains additional "Mmm Good" recipes—more than thirty—to help you mix your meal plans and exercise routines to reach your fat-loss goals. But this time I've got favorites from some helpful "boot campers" from my Central Florida gym, plus a few from avid readers who just couldn't help being honorary chefs for a day. I think you'll enjoy making these recipes as much as my staff and I did whipping them up—and tasting them.

Along with each recipe, you'll find a list of the dish's protein, carb, and fat content. Equally important, each recipe is coded to a corresponding planner so you will know if it is OK to substitute for a particular day. The codes are the same as those explained in Chapter 3:

- Planner A recipes are for deplete days.
- Planner B recipes are for baseline days.
- Planner C recipes are for carb-down days.

- Planner D recipes are for carb-up days.
- MIC recipes are for the metabolic increase cycle.
- MAC recipes are for the metabolic adaptation cycle.

The codes make it easy for busy readers to scan the chapters for the recipes they need, making menu planning a breeze. I've also provided advice to making cooking quicker and easier.

So read on, eat up, and enjoy more of my "Mmm Good" recipes!

Conquer the Code

If cooking isn't your thing and these are the first recipes you've ever tried, try to make it your thing. One reason Americans have gotten overweight is our easy reliance on frozen, precooked, or premade food. Learning to cook fresh ingredients for your own meals is one of the joys of conquering the fat-loss code.

Quick-Fix Tips and Ideas

- Use chopped, prewashed lettuce in a bag for quick salads.
- Top salads with grape tomatoes—no cutting necessary. Just wash them and pile them on.
- Canned chicken and tuna is ready to eat. Open the can and flake it into tomato halves.
- Use your Crock-Pot to make beef tips with broccoli in gravy or chicken in tomato sauce. Either one can stew all day and be ready to eat when you get home from work.
- Use canned veggies—drain them and season with olive oil and fresh garlic.

- Check to see if your supermarket carries freshly cooked rotisserie chicken and turkey breast. If so, all you need to do is stop in on your way home and pick up your main course.
- Cook a lot of food at once, portion it into freezer bags, and freeze.
- When you order food in a restaurant, take part of it home for another meal.
- Keep protein powder in a shaker cup with you at all times. When you can't grab a meal, you can add it to water or some other beverage for a quick substitute.
- When ordering roast beef or turkey breast at the deli, ask the server to put paper between specific weight portions, such as every 4 ounces.

10

Breakfast and Egg Recipes

Egg White Poppers

These snacks are very popular with bodybuilders who take them to the gym in plastic resealable bags and pop them while working out to get an extra protein boost.

Use planners A, B, C, D, MIC, MAC

Cooking spray

Enough egg whites to fill a plastic ice cube tray

Coat an ice cube tray with cooking spray. Pour the egg whites in and microwave on high for 4 minutes. Refrigerate for 1 hour.

You can experiment by mixing a small amount of sugar-free powdered Kool-Aid or Jell-O® gelatin into egg whites to add flavor.

Makes 12 poppers

Nutritional Value
Protein: 3 grams per popper
Fat: 0 grams
Carbs: 0 grams

Rolled Egg White Omelet with Mushrooms

Use planners A, B, C, D, MIC, MAC

> 2 tablespoons salted butter, melted
>
> 2 teaspoons minced shallot
>
> Pinch of fresh thyme
>
> ½ cup sliced mushrooms, any kind
>
> Salt and pepper to taste
>
> 4 large egg whites

Preheat broiler. Heat 1 tablespoon butter in a medium nonstick, ovenproof skillet. Add the shallot and thyme, and cook over medium heat, stirring constantly, until fragrant, about 30 seconds. Add the mushrooms, season with salt and pepper, and cook over medium-high heat until mushrooms are tender and lightly browned, about 5 minutes.

Whisk eggs until frothy. Season with salt and pepper and beat in remaining 1 tablespoon butter. Pour the beaten egg whites into the skillet and cook over medium heat until almost opaque, drawing in the edges of the omelet with a spatula as they set and tilting the pan to allow the uncooked whites to run underneath, about 40 seconds. Transfer the skillet to the oven and broil about 10 seconds, or until the top is just set. Run the spatula around the edge of the omelet to release it. Fold one third of the omelet onto itself, and then roll it out onto a plate so it is oval in shape. Serve at once.

Makes 1 serving

Nutritional Value
Protein: 15 grams
Fat: 7 grams
Carbs: 3 grams

Protein Oatmeal

Use planners B, C, D, MIC, MAC

> 1 serving quick or old-fashioned oats
>
> 5 egg whites, or equivalent in liquid eggs ("100% egg whites")
>
> 2 packets Splenda or low-sugar jam or cinnamon to taste

Prepare oats according to package directions; however, add egg whites to water prior to adding oats. Cook until done. Add Splenda, or stir in low-sugar jam or cinnamon.

Makes 1 serving

Nutritional Value
Protein: 17 grams
Fat: 1 gram
Carbs: 25 grams

Fake French Toast

This tastes more like a pancake than French toast, but it's great, especially with maple syrup. If you find it difficult to flip, cut it in half.

Use planners B, D, MAC

> 2 eggs
>
> 4 tablespoons ricotta cheese (or cream cheese)
>
> Dash of cinnamon
>
> Dash of nutmeg
>
> 2 packets Splenda (optional)
>
> 1 tablespoon butter

Combine eggs, ricotta cheese, cinnamon, nutmeg, and Splenda (if using) in a medium bowl; set aside. Melt butter in a small skillet; pour in batter, spreading a little. Brown on one side, flip, and brown on the other side.

Makes 1 large serving

Nutritional Value
Protein: 18 grams
Fat: 17 grams
Carbs: 4 grams

Super-Healthy Pancakes

I like to make 1 big pancake, but you can make them any size you'd like.

Use planners B, C, D, MIC, MAC

4 to 5 egg whites

½ cup old-fashioned oatmeal

¼ cup low-fat cottage cheese

½ scoop vanilla or plain protein powder

Dash of cinnamon

Cooking spray

Sugar-free maple syrup or sugar-free jam

In a medium bowl or blender, combine the egg whites, oatmeal, cottage cheese, protein powder, and cinnamon. Coat a medium skillet with cooking spray. Add batter to pan and cook until set; flip and cook other side

Serve with syrup or jam.

Makes 1 serving

Nutritional Value
Protein: 30 grams
Fat: 3 grams
Carbs: 25 grams

Low-Carb Pancakes

Use planners B and D

> ½ cup vanilla protein powder
>
> ½ cup ricotta cheese
>
> 2 tablespoons heavy cream
>
> 2 packets Splenda (optional)
>
> 2 large eggs
>
> 2 teaspoons baking powder
>
> Dash of cinnamon
>
> Dash of nutmeg
>
> Water for consistency
>
> Cooking spray

In a medium bowl, combine the protein powder, ricotta cheese, cream, Splenda (if using), eggs, baking power, cinnamon, and nutmeg. Start adding water slowly until the batter reaches a fairly thin consistency. Coat a medium skillet with cooking spray and heat over medium heat. When the pan is hot, spoon the batter in and spread a little. Cook the pancakes until bubbly on one side; flip and cook a few minutes more.

Makes 2 servings

Nutritional Value
Protein: 26 grams
Fat: 29 grams
Carbs: 6 grams

11

Shakes and Smoothies

Cinnamon Roll Smoothie

Use planners A, B, C, D

> 1 scoop vanilla or chocolate protein powder
>
> ¼ cup heavy whipping cream
>
> ¾ cup water
>
> ¼ teaspoon cinnamon
>
> 2 tablespoons Butter Buds (optional)
>
> 1 packet Splenda (optional)
>
> ¼ cup ice (optional)

Combine all ingredients in a blender and pulse until well mixed. Pour into a tall glass.

Makes 1 serving

Nutritional Value
The nutritional values will vary according to the kind of protein powder you use, so check the label.

Chocolate Raspberry Protein Shake

Try coffee instead of Crystal Light® for another shake idea.
Use planners A, B, C, D

> 8 to 10 ounces prepared raspberry Crystal Light drink
>
> 4 to 10 ice cubes (fewer for thinner consistency, more for thicker shake)
>
> 1 to 1½ scoops chocolate protein powder

Pour the prepared Crystal Light into a blender. Add the desired amount of ice and protein powder, and then blend until smooth. Drink immediately or put in the freezer to thicken.

Makes 1 serving

Nutritional Value
The nutritional values will vary according to the kind of protein powder you use, so check the label.

Orange Dream Protein Shake

Use planners A, B, C, D

> 8 to 10 ounces prepared orange-pineapple Crystal
> Light drink
>
> 4 to 10 ice cubes (fewer for thinner consistency,
> more for thicker shake)
>
> 1 to 1½ scoops vanilla protein powder

Pour the prepared Crystal Light into a blender. Add the desired amount of ice and protein powder; blend until smooth. Drink immediately, or put in the freezer to thicken.

Makes 1 serving

Nutritional Value
The nutritional values will vary according to the kind of protein powder you use, so check the label.

Mocha Protein Shake

Use planners A, B, C, D

> 8 to 10 ounces water
>
> 1 heaping teaspoon instant coffee (regular or decaf)
>
> 4 to 10 ice cubes (fewer for thinner consistency,
>   more for thicker shake)
>
> 1 to 1½ scoops chocolate protein powder

Pour the water in a blender. Add the rest of the ingredients and blend until smooth. Drink immediately, or put in the freezer to thicken.

Makes 1 serving

Nutritional Value
The nutritional values will vary according to the kind of protein powder you use, so check the label.

Chocolate Banana Protein Shake

Use planners D and MAC

8 ounces skim milk

1 scoop chocolate protein powder

½ banana, frozen

3 ice cubes

1 tablespoon peanut butter

Pour all ingredients in a blender; blend until well combined.

Makes 1 serving

Nutritional Value
Protein: Varies according to
    the kind of protein powder
    used (Check the label.)
Fat: 7 grams
Carbs: 10 grams

Yogurt Smoothie

You can also use flavored yogurt in this recipe.
Use planners D and MAC

⅓ cup plain low-fat or nonfat yogurt

¼ cup fresh or frozen pineapple or peaches

½ cup egg whites

Place all ingredients in a blender and mix for 10 to 15 seconds.

Makes 1 serving

Nutritional Value
Protein: 15 grams
Fat: 7 grams
Carbs: 22 grams

Fruit Smoothie

Use planners B, C, D, MIC, MAC

> 1 scoop protein powder
>
> ½ ripe banana
>
> ¼ cup fresh or frozen blueberries
>
> ¼ cup fresh or frozen strawberries
>
> 1 cup orange juice
>
> 3 to 4 ice cubes

Place all ingredients in a blender and mix for 45 seconds until smooth.

Makes 1 serving

Nutritional Value
The nutritional values will vary according to the kind of protein powder you use, so check the label.

12

Soups and Salads

Cabbage Soup

This recipe was submitted by Denise Beaulieu.
Use planners B, C, D, MIC, MAC

2 cans low-sodium chicken broth

1 medium head cabbage, chopped

5 whole black peppercorns

2 cloves garlic left whole

Combine all ingredients in a stockpot and cook for 2 to 3 hours.

Makes 6 servings

Nutritional Value
Protein: 3 grams
Fat: 5 grams
Carbs: 12 grams

Lentil Bean Soup

Use planners D and MAC

2 tablespoons olive oil

1 onion, chopped

½ cup chopped carrot

1 cup chopped celery

1 cup lentils, washed

4 cups low-sodium chicken stock

4 cups water

¼ cup tomato puree

4 teaspoons fresh thyme, or 2 teaspoons dried
    thyme

1 clove garlic, crushed

Salt and freshly ground black pepper to taste

Heat the oil in a large pot over medium-high heat. Add the onion and sauté until brown. Add the carrot and celery; sauté for 5 minutes. Add the lentils, chicken stock, water, tomato puree, thyme, and garlic; bring to a boil. Reduce heat to medium. Cover and cook for 1 hour. Season the soup to taste with salt and pepper.

Makes 8 to 10 servings

Nutritional Value
Protein: 7 grams
Fat: 18 grams
Carbs: 28 grams

Butternut Squash Soup

Use planners B, D, MAC

3 pounds butternut squash, halved with seeds scooped out

3 tablespoons unsalted butter, cut into 6 pieces

Salt and black pepper to taste

2 tablespoons olive oil

1 medium onion, chopped

2 quarts low-sodium chicken stock

2 teaspoons fresh thyme

1 bay leaf

2 tablespoons heavy whipping cream

Preheat oven to 400°F. Place the squash on a baking sheet, cut side up. Place a piece of butter in each half and season with salt and pepper. Roast the squash for 45 minutes, or until tender.

Scoop the squash out of the skins into a bowl; set aside. In a large, heavy stockpot, heat the olive oil. Add the onion and more salt and pepper, and cook over medium heat, stirring until softened, about 5 minutes. Stir in the squash, chicken stock, thyme, and bay leaf; bring to a boil over high heat, stirring frequently. Reduce heat and simmer the soup for 15 minutes.

Remove the bay leaf. Working in batches, puree the soup in a blender or food processor. Return it to the pot and add the heavy cream. Season to taste with salt and pepper.

Makes 6 to 8 servings

Nutritional Value
Protein: 6 grams
Fat: 6 grams
Carbs: 20 grams

Italian Roasted Pepper Soup

This recipe was submitted by Jackie Butler. Roasted red peppers can be found in most supermarkets. This recipe is great for days when you can have pasta, and it can easily be halved. Add ½ cup of low-sodium Knudsen vegetable juice to kick the flavor up a notch without adding too many carbs and calories. Sprinkle croutons on top when you have company.

Use planners B, D, MAC

1 8-ounce package fresh white mushrooms, sliced

2 tablespoons water

2 7-ounce jars roasted red peppers, including liquid

2 small cans ready-to-serve, low-fat, low-sodium chicken broth

1 teaspoon crushed Italian seasoning

1 teaspoon garlic powder

1 teaspoon onion powder

8 ounces fresh cheese tortellini

In a large saucepan, cook the mushrooms and water, stirring occasionally, until the mushrooms are slightly softened, 3 to 4 minutes. Meanwhile, place the red peppers and their liquid in a food processor and blend until smooth, about 30 seconds. Add to the mushrooms along with the chicken broth, Italian seasoning, garlic powder, and onion powder; bring to a boil and cook, uncovered, about 10 minutes. Add the tortellini and cook until tender, another 10 minutes.

Makes 6 servings

Nutritional Value
Protein: 5 grams
Fat: 6 grams
Carbs: 22 grams

Taco Salad

Use planners B, C, D, MAC

> 12 ounces ground beef, lean if desired
>
> 2 teaspoons taco seasoning mix
>
> 4 cups shredded lettuce
>
> 4 ounces cheddar cheese, shredded
>
> 4 tablespoons salsa
>
> 2 tablespoons sour cream

In a medium skillet over medium heat, brown the beef. Stir in the seasoning mix; set aside. Divide the lettuce onto two plates. Top each with half the ground beef mixture, sprinkle with cheese, and then top with salsa and sour cream.

Makes 2 servings

Nutritional Value
Protein: 12 grams
Fat: 67 grams
Carbs: 8 grams

Egg Salad

This salad can be served rolled in lettuce leaves or scooped into celery stalks.

Use planners A, B, C, D, MIC, MAC

1 whole egg plus 2 to 3 egg whites, hard-boiled and chopped

1 tablespoon mayonnaise

Diced onion to taste

Diced celery to taste

Combine all ingredients. This is best if refrigerated before eating.

Makes 1 serving

Nutritional Value
Protein: 15 to 18 grams
Fat: 7 grams
Carbs: 3 grams

Tuna Salad

This salad can be served rolled in lettuce leaves or scooped into celery stalks.

Use planners A, B, C, D, MAC

> 1 6-ounce packet albacore tuna
>
> 1 whole egg (or egg whites if preferred), hard-boiled and chopped
>
> 1 tablespoon mayonnaise
>
> 1 onion, diced
>
> Diced celery to taste
>
> Dash of sage

Combine all ingredients.

Makes 2 servings

Nutritional Value
Protein: 28 grams
Fat: 3 grams
Carbs: 0 grams

13

Sides and Vegetables

Roasted Asparagus with Feta

You can use Parmesan cheese instead of feta if you prefer.
   Use planners B, D, MIC, MAC

> 2½ medium asparagus, ends trimmed
>
> 2 tablespoons olive oil
>
> ½ teaspoon salt
>
> ½ teaspoon ground black pepper
>
> ½ cup crumbled feta cheese

Preheat oven to 400°F. Lay the asparagus in a single layer in a baking pan. Toss with olive oil, salt, and pepper. Roast until tender, about 12 minutes. Sprinkle with feta and roast another 2 minutes.

Makes 1 serving

Nutritional Value
Protein: 2 grams
Fat: 7 grams
Carbs: 12 grams

Broccoli Italiano

Use planners B, C, D, MAC

>Water
>
>5½ cups broccoli florets
>
>½ cup thinly sliced green onion
>
>4 teaspoons olive oil (or flaxseed oil)
>
>4 garlic cloves, minced
>
>2 tablespoons lemon juice
>
>½ teaspoon salt
>
>¼ teaspoon black pepper
>
>2 large fresh mushrooms, sliced

Cover the bottom of a large saucepan with 1 inch of water; bring to a boil. Place the broccoli in a steamer basket over the water. Cover and steam for 4 to 5 minutes, or until crisp tender. Meanwhile, in a nonstick skillet, cook the onion in oil over medium heat for 1 minute. Add the garlic; cook 30 seconds longer. Reduce the heat and add the broccoli, lemon juice, salt, and pepper. Toss to coat. Remove from heat; let stand 5 minutes before serving. Add mushrooms to garnish.

Makes 1 serving

Nutritional Value
Protein: 2 grams
Fat: 3 grams
Carbs: 5 grams

Broccoli with Lemon Sauce

Use planners D and MAC

> ¼ cup slivered almonds
>
> 2 teaspoons butter
>
> 2 pounds fresh broccoli, cut into spears
>
> 2 teaspoons water
>
> 3 ounces shredded cheese
>
> ¼ cup skim milk
>
> 1 teaspoon lemon juice
>
> ½ teaspoon ground ginger

Combine the almonds and butter and divide among 6 ramekins. Microwave on high for 2 to 3 minutes, or until almonds are light brown. Set aside. Peel the stalk of each broccoli spear. Arrange in a shallow 1½ quart microwave-safe casserole dish, with the stalks toward the outside of the dish. Sprinkle with water and cover tightly. Microwave on high for 5 minutes. Rearrange the broccoli, moving the stalks to the center of the dish. Recover; microwave on high for 5 to 7 minutes, or until crisp tender. Let stand 5 minutes.

In a 2-cup glass measure, microwave the cheese at 30 percent power (medium-low) for 1 minute, or until softened. Stir until smooth. Beat in the milk, lemon juice, and ginger. Microwave at 50 percent power (medium) for 1 minute, or until hot. Drain the broccoli and top with the sauce. Sprinkle with toasted almonds.

Makes 6 servings

Nutritional Value
Protein: 8 grams
Fat: 8 grams
Carbs: 10 grams

Horseradish Sauce for Veggies

Use planners B, D, MAC

       1 cup reduced-fat sour cream

       2 teaspoons prepared horseradish

       2 teaspoons Dijon mustard

       ¼ teaspoon salt

       ¼ teaspoon black pepper

In a small saucepan, combine all ingredients. Cook and stir over medium-low heat until heated through. Serve immediately.

Makes 6 serving (2 tablespoons each)

Nutritional Value
Protein: 2 grams
Fat: 3 grams
Carbs: 2 grams

Zucchini Frittata

Use planners B, D, MAC

1 tablespoon olive oil

1 medium onion, chopped

2 cloves garlic, pressed or minced

2 medium zucchini, sliced (about 3 cups)

Salt and black pepper to taste

4 large eggs (or 3 whole and 3 whites)

2 tablespoons finely chopped fresh basil

2 tablespoons minced flat-leaf Italian parsley

2 tablespoons Parmesan cheese

Heat ½ tablespoon of the oil in a 10-inch, heavy-bottomed, ovenproof skillet. Add the onion and sauté until tender and translucent. Stir in the garlic and zucchini; continue sautéing until the zucchini is just tender. Season with salt and pepper and remove from heat; set aside. In a mixing bowl, whisk together the eggs, basil, and parsley. Stir in the sautéed vegetables. Add the remaining ½ tablespoon of oil to the same skillet over medium heat, tilting the pan to coat the bottom and sides. Add the egg-vegetable mixture, spreading evenly. Reduce heat to low and cover the pan. Cook for 10 to 15 minutes, until set. Preheat the broiler. Sprinkle grated cheese on top of the frittata, and broil briefly until lightly browned. Cut into 3 wedges. Serve immediately from the pan or transfer to a large round plate or platter.

Makes 3 servings

Nutritional Value
Protein: 2 grams
Fat: 12 grams
Carbs: 22 grams

Ballyhoo Zucchini

This recipe works best with fresh Parmesan cheese.
Use planners B, D, MIC, MAC

> 1½ pounds zucchini, coarsely chopped
> (about 4 cups)
>
> ½ teaspoon salt
>
> 2 eggs
>
> 6 tablespoons Parmesan cheese
>
> ½ clove garlic, minced
>
> ¼ cup butter

Combine the zucchini and salt in a medium bowl. Let stand for 15 minutes. Squeeze the zucchini with your hands to press out moisture. Stir in the eggs, cheese, and garlic. Melt 2 tablespoons of the butter in a large frying pan over medium-high heat. Mound about 2 tablespoons of the zucchini mixture in the pan; flatten slightly to make a patty. Repeat until the pan is filled, but don't crowd the patties. Cook them, turning once, until golden on both sides (about 6 minutes total). Lift out the patties and arrange on paper towels on a warm platter. Repeat until the remaining zucchini mixture has been used up, adding more butter to the pan as needed.

Makes 8 servings

Nutritional Value
Protein: 2 grams
Fat: 7 grams
Carbs: 12 grams

Asparagus in Vinaigrette with Pecans and Bacon

Use planners D and MAC

> 1 tablespoon olive oil
>
> 1 tablespoon minced fresh garlic
>
> 1½ pounds asparagus, sliced into 1½-inch pieces
>
> 2 tablespoons balsamic vinegar
>
> 2 teaspoons sugar substitute
>
> 1½ teaspoons minced fresh tarragon
>
> ¾ teaspoon salt
>
> 1 teaspoon black pepper
>
> 2 tablespoons chopped pecans, toasted
>
> 2 bacon slices, cooked and crumbled

Heat the oil in a large nonstick skillet over medium-high heat. Add the garlic and sauté for 1 minute. Add the asparagus; sauté for 4 minutes or until tender. Meanwhile, combine the vinegar and sugar substitute in a small bowl. Add the vinegar mixture, tarragon, salt, and pepper to the asparagus; stir well. Cook 2 minutes, stirring frequently. Sprinkle with the pecans and bacon.

Makes 4 servings

Nutritional Value
Protein: 5 grams
Fat: 7 grams
Carbs: 11 grams

Grilled Vegetables

Use planners B, D, MIC, MAC

Marinade

> ½ cup cilantro leaves
>
> 3 cloves garlic, peeled
>
> ¼ cup dried cranberries
>
> ½ teaspoon garam masala
>
> 1½ tablespoons lemon juice
>
> ½ cup olive oil
>
> ½ cup water
>
> 1 teaspoon sea salt
>
> 1 teaspoon freshly ground black pepper

Vegetables

> 2 medium summer squash, sliced into ⅜-inch-thick strips
>
> 1 medium eggplant, sliced into ⅜-inch-thick strips
>
> Cooking spray

Combine all marinade ingredients and brush on the vegetables; allow to rest 15 to 30 minutes. Prep the grill until it's hot. Lay the vegetable slices on the grill and cook for a few minutes. Check for grill marks, then turn. Complete grilling and keep warm.

Makes 4 to 6 servings

Nutritional Value
Protein: 5 grams
Fat: 3 grams
Carbs: 20 grams

Stuffed Pepper Cups

Use planners B, D, MAC

6 medium green peppers

1 pound lean ground beef

⅓ cup chopped sweet onion

½ teaspoon salt

Black pepper to taste

1 16-ounce can crushed tomatoes

½ cup uncooked long-grain rice

½ cup water

1 teaspoon Worcestershire sauce

4 ounces sharp cheddar cheese, shredded

Preheat oven to 350°F. Cut off the tops of the green peppers, remove the seeds and membrane, and scallop the edges if desired. Precook the peppers in boiling, salted water for 5 minutes. (For crisp peppers, omit precooking.)

In a medium skillet, brown the meat and onion; add salt and black pepper. Stir in the tomatoes, rice, water, and Worcestershire sauce. Cover and simmer 15 minutes. Stir in the cheese. Fill the peppers with the mixture and place in a baking dish. Bake for 20 to 25 minutes.

Makes 6 servings

Nutritional Value
Protein: 15 grams
Fat: 10 grams
Carbs: 11 grams

14

Entrees

Moist Broiled Salmon

Use planners B, C, D

> 1½ pounds skinless salmon, cut into 4 pieces
>
> Salt to taste
>
> Freshly ground pepper to taste
>
> 1½ tablespoons olive oil
>
> 1 small red or yellow onion, cut into ⅛-inch slices

Preheat broiler to medium-high. Season the salmon pieces with salt and pepper and lightly brush with half the oil. Place onion slices over fish and season again with salt, pepper, and oil.

Place under the broiler and cook 12 to 15 minutes until done.

Makes 4 servings

Nutritional Value
Protein: 20 grams
Fat: 10 grams
Carbs: 5 grams

Five-Alarm Chili

You can use 8 ounces of mushrooms, chopped, instead of the pinto beans to avoid carbohydrates. To make veggie five-alarm chili, omit the ground beef and replace with 1 red onion and 8 ounces mushrooms, chopped.

Use planners D and MAC

1 pound lean ground beef, chicken, or turkey

1 onion, chopped

1 clove garlic, minced

1 green pepper, seeded and chopped

1 teaspoon oregano

½ teaspoon cumin

½ teaspoon freshly ground black pepper

½ teaspoon cayenne pepper, or to taste

1 14-ounce can pinto beans, drained

1 28-ounce can sodium-free diced tomatoes

In a nonstick Dutch oven or stockpot, brown the ground meat, onion, garlic, and green pepper over medium heat until the meat is fully cooked. Drain off the excess oil. Add the oregano, cumin, black pepper, cayenne pepper, and beans. Stir together for 1 minute. Add the tomatoes and bring to a boil. Lower heat and simmer on low for 10 to 15 minutes, stirring occasionally.

Makes 6 servings

Nutritional Value (with beans)
Protein: 16 grams
Fat: 6 grams
Carbs: 21 grams

Nutritional Value (with mushrooms)
Protein: 13 grams
Fat: 6 grams
Carbs: 11 grams

Chicken Cacciatore

On a carb-up day, pour this mixture over ½ cup cooked rice. Use planners B, D, MIC, MAC

8 ounces chicken, cut into pieces

1 to 2 tablespoons olive oil

1 garlic clove, minced

2 tablespoons diced green onion

⅛ teaspoon thyme

½ teaspoon dried basil

¼ to ½ cup tomato paste

½ to 1 cup sliced mushrooms

Salt and black pepper to taste

1¼ cups chicken broth

1 bay leaf

In a large skillet, brown the chicken in olive oil with garlic and green onion. Add the rest of the ingredients and simmer until the chicken is tender, about 45 minutes. Keep checking to make sure the mixture retains plenty of liquid; add more chicken broth if needed.

Makes 4 serving

Nutritional Value
Protein: 32 grams
Fat: 3 grams
Carbs: 10 grams

Spicy Cajun Chicken

Use planners B, C, D, MAC

4 4- to 6-ounce chicken breasts

¼ teaspoon salt

1 small can chicken broth

2 teaspoons curry powder

2 teaspoons crushed dried oregano

2 cloves garlic, crushed

1 teaspoon dry mustard

1 teaspoon Worcestershire sauce

¼ teaspoon hot pepper sauce

Preheat oven to 375°F. Arrange the chicken breasts in a single layer in a shallow baking dish; season with salt and set aside. Whisk together the rest of the ingredients until well combined. Pour over the chicken and bake, uncovered, turning once, until thoroughly cooked, about 25 minutes.

Makes 4 servings

Nutritional Value
Protein: 25 grams
Fat: 3 grams
Carbs: 5 grams

Salmon Patties

This recipe was submitted by Frances Summers. Instead of bread crumbs, like my mother used to use, the egg holds the patty together, making this a nice low-carb dish. Tuna also works well if you don't want salmon; substitute dill for basil and use a Mrs. Dash spice instead of salmon seasoning.

Use planners B, C, D, MIC, MAC

1 small can boneless, skinless salmon

2 teaspoons Chef Paul Prudhomme's Salmon Magic® seasoning blend (or you can use any Mrs. Dash mixed seasoning)

1 tablespoon chopped fresh basil

1 whole egg (or 2 egg whites), lightly beaten

Cooking spray

In a bowl, combine the salmon, seasoning, and basil. Slowly add egg (or egg white, if using) until the consistency allows you to form firm patties. Coat a medium skillet with cooking spray and fry the patties for 3 to 4 minutes on each side. (Salmon does not need to be recooked and will get dry if cooked too long.)

Makes 1 serving

Nutritional Value
Protein: 28 grams
Fat: 3 grams
Carbs: 5 grams

Citrus Tilapia

Use planners B, D, MIC, MAC

  2 tablespoons olive oil

  ¼ cup fresh orange juice

  1 tablespoon orange zest

  1 teaspoon crushed red pepper flakes

  Salt to taste

  Freshly ground black pepper to taste

  4 6- to 8-ounce tilapia fillets, rinsed and patted dry

Preheat oven to 400°F. Combine the olive oil, orange juice, orange zest, red pepper flakes, salt, and black pepper in a shallow baking dish. Add the tilapia and coat both sides of fillets with the seasoning. Bake 10 to 12 minutes until fish is done.

Makes 4 servings

Nutritional Value
Protein: 24 grams
Fat: 10 grams
Carbs: 10 grams

Turkey Mishmash

This recipe was submitted by Denise Beaulieu. It is delicious!
Use planners B, C, D

> 1 clove garlic, peeled
>
> 1 tablespoon olive oil
>
> 5 or 6 whole mushrooms, sliced
>
> ½ yellow squash, diced
>
> ½ zucchini, diced
>
> 8 ounces ground turkey
>
> Salt to taste
>
> Black pepper to taste
>
> ⅛ teaspoon onion powder
>
> ½ medium head green cabbage, shredded
>
> ½ cup low-sodium chicken broth

In a large skillet, sauté garlic clove in olive oil; add the mushrooms, yellow squash, and zucchini; cook until soft. Add the ground turkey, salt, pepper, and onion powder, and brown until the meat is cooked thoroughly. Remove from heat.

In a large skillet, sear the cabbage until it starts to brown. Toss and add small amounts of chicken broth. Sauté until the cabbage is very soft.

Put cabbage on plates with turkey mishmash on top.

Makes 2 servings

Nutritional Value
Protein: 20 grams
Fat: 3 grams
Carbs: 12 grams

15

Desserts

Creamy Jell-O Dessert

Use planners B, D, MIC, MAC

1¼ cups water

1 small package sugar-free Jell-O, any flavor

½ cup heavy cream

Boil 1 cup of the water and mix into the Jell-O; stir until Jell-O is dissolved. Divide among 4 dishes and chill until set. Combine the remaining water and cream; add to Jell-O.

Makes 4 servings

Nutritional Value
Protein: 5 grams
Fat: 7 grams
Carbs: 2 grams

Simplest Fruit Cobbler

You can serve this dessert topped with vanilla yogurt, whipped cream, or ice cream.

Use planners D and MAC

Cobbler Topping

⅓ cup rolled oats

⅓ cup unbleached all-purpose flour

⅓ cup sugarcane crystals

⅓ cup pecans

¼ teaspoon cinnamon

3 tablespoons unsalted butter, cold

1 tablespoon vegetable oil, preferably canola or
    safflower

Fruit

1¼ pounds fresh fruit of choice, pitted and sliced

⅓ cup dried apricots or peaches, sliced

Preheat oven to 400°F. In a food processor combine all topping ingredients; pulse until mixture is crumbly. Place the fresh and dried fruit in a 6-cup gratin or baking dish, and then sprinkle the cobbler topping on top. Bake uncovered for about 40 minutes, until browned on top. Cool until just warm, and serve with your choice of topping.

Makes 4 servings

Nutritional Value
Protein: 7 grams
Fat: 12 grams
Carbs: 28 grams

What the Code Crackers Are Saying

Jerri Griffee

This program has begun a new life for me. I've been fat since I was three years old and morbidly obese for as long as I can remember. As every overweight person has, I've gone the route of every program on the market: support groups, therapy, hypnosis (twice), shots and pills, and whatever else made sense at the moment. I never lasted more than six months and always gained the weight back.

Any plan will work if you can continue to follow it. The problem was that I always lost interest or hit a plateau and gave up, but I can follow Wendy's plan. I've lost seventy-five pounds so far in the sixteen months since I started the program, and I'm still doing it. I've lost thirteen inches just from my waist, and I'm wearing the same size clothing that I wore when I was thirteen years old! (I'm forty-nine now.) My blood sugar, cholesterol level, blood pressure, and stamina are all amazing.

My college education is in food and nutrition. I spent many years managing dietary departments in several health care facilities, so I "knew" every-thing (or so I thought). Wendy's nutritional and medical science information blew me away. She taught me how the body actually uses food and how to "train" the body to find the fat and get rid of it.

Wendy inspires me. Her plan makes sense, and best of all, it's doable. I'm not going to lie and say that you can eat whatever you want, whenever you want. There is no such thing as a "miracle diet," but Wendy works her patterns so that you can enjoy your life. There was no suffering during the holidays or even on a fifteen-night cruise I took recently. I have no regrets with what I ate or didn't eat and was still able to lose weight and inches.

Appendix

Beginner's Home Workout

Weight Training and Exercise

For beginners, I suggest doing one set of 10 to 12 repetitions for each of the following workouts, using dumbbells that are between 5 and 8 pounds. If this is too hard, start with the 5-pound weight and do fewer reps, and then work your way up. If this is too easy for you, use 8-pound weights and increase the number of repetitions or sets until you feel challenged but not exhausted or in pain. Your workouts should be based on what your body can handle. Remember to consult your health care or fitness professional before starting any exercise program.

Abs

Crunches

Lie on your back with your knees bent. Curl your upper body toward your knees until your shoulder blades and upper back clear the floor.

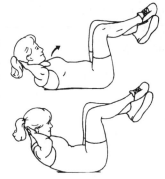

Chest

Bench Fly

Lie on your back with your arms above you and slightly bent. Lower your arms out to the side until the weights are at shoulder level with your palms facing upward. Raise them back to the starting position.

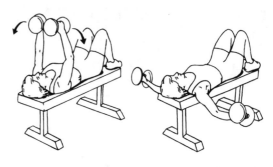

Bench Press

Lie on your back and start with the dumbbells at chest level. Press up until your arms are straight. Lower back to starting position.

Back

One Arm Bent-Over Row

From starting position, pull the right dumbbell to the side of your chest. Complete all repetitions on the right side, and then repeat on the left.

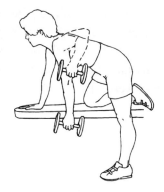

Upright Row (Traps)

Stand with your feet together, holding the dumbbells in front of your thighs. Keeping the weights close together, pull them up to your chin, keeping your elbows high.

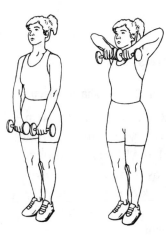

Shoulders

Seated Press

Sit with your palms facing your ears; press to straight arm position. Rotate your hands so the palms face forward at the top of the movement.

Arms

Bent-Over Kickback (Triceps)

Raise your right arm backward until your elbow locks in a straight position. Lower slowly back to the starting position. Repeat with the left arm.

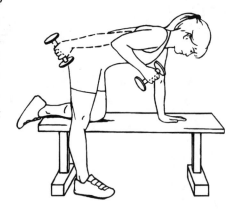

Standing One-Arm Extension (Triceps)

Using one arm to brace, rotate lower arm upward to the straight arm position. Complete all repetitions to one side. Repeat to other side.

Standing Alternating Curl (Biceps)

Stand with your arms at your sides, palms facing forward. Keeping your upper arms close to your body, curl the right dumbbell up to your shoulder, and then lower it back to the straight arm position. Repeat with the left arm.

Legs

Lunge (Glutes)

Stand with your legs shoulder-width apart, your head up, and your back straight. Step your right foot forward in a lunge, bending your legs until your right thigh is parallel to the floor. Return to the starting position and repeat on the left side.

Weighted Kickback (Glutes)

Kneel on all fours. Bring your right leg forward, tucking your knee to your chest. Drive the leg back and up until it's straight and slightly above the rest of your body. Complete all repetitions to the right, and then repeat on the left side.

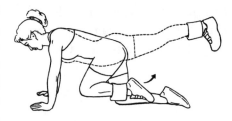

Standing Heel Raise (Calves)

Standing on a board with your knees locked, raise yourself up on your toes as high as possible.

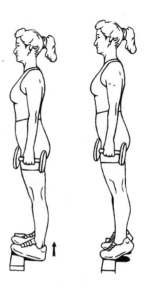

Types of Cardio Training

Low Intensity, Long Duration

- This involves aerobic work done at around 40 to 60 percent of your maximum heart rate.
- Low-intensity cardio is slow, easy, continuous, and long; it can be done for more than forty minutes. Some examples are walking, cycling, and jogging.
- You should be able to converse comfortably while exercising (called the talk test).
- This type of training is good for people who are just starting cardio work.
- It is reasonably good for fat loss, especially for very obese people.
- It is the least demanding form of aerobic training.

Medium Intensity, Medium Duration

- This involves aerobic work done at around 70 percent of your maximum heart rate.
- This type of exercise is more difficult, so you cannot sustain the workout as long; a session is usually twenty to forty minutes. Spinning would be a good example.
- This type of training can be used for fat loss and for increasing aerobic capacity.
- It is characterized by heavy breathing but not so much that you are soon out of breath and must stop.

High Intensity, Short Duration

- This involves aerobic work done at around 80 to 85 percent of your maximum heart rate. Eighty-five percent of the maximum heart rate is generally considered to be the *anaerobic threshold*, though this can vary depending on genetics and fitness level.
- This is a very demanding form of training, so it can be done for only about five to twenty minutes, depending on fitness level.

Aerobic Interval Training

- You should alternate your heart rate from all-out sprinting at 95 percent max back down to 75 percent max.
- Interval training involves alternating periods of moderate- to high-intensity aerobic exercise with rest periods of low-intensity exercise, such as three minutes of fast running followed by one minute of slow walking, repeated four times.
- You can vary the intervals and intensities to your liking; for example, ten minutes of moderate work, two minutes easy, one minute hard, or perhaps five minutes hard, five minutes easy.
- The key is variation and not working so hard that you must stop completely.

Anaerobic Interval Training

- This involves exercise done at 85 to 100 percent of your maximum heart rate.
- This type of training involves working hard for short periods of time, and then resting for equal or longer periods of time. An example would be sprinting as hard as you can for thirty seconds, walking for thirty seconds, sprinting for another thirty seconds, and so on. This cycle might be repeated three to six times, depending on your fitness level.

Fartlek Training

- Translated from Swedish, *fartlek* means "speed play."
- For this type of cardio, you mix all of the previously mentioned types of training together in one session. You might run for ten minutes, sprint for thirty seconds, walk for two minutes, run fast for two minutes, jog slowly for five minutes, and then sprint again.
- This is a good way to work through the entire intensity spectrum as well as to prevent boredom.

Circuit Training

- Circuit training is basically aerobic weight training.
- You set up a number of stations with a variety of exercises that work your entire body, such as a bench for arm exercises and a mat for abdominal curls. You can also mix in treadmill work, rope-skipping, cycling, and so on to add variety.
- Use fairly light weights that you can lift easily.
- Do each exercise continuously for a specified time interval, such as one minute at each station. Go through the cycle one to three times (see the section Sample Circuit Training Workout for a suggested order of activities). You can build up to more time per activity as you get stronger.

- This is a reasonably good way to do aerobic work and weight training at the same time.
- It also has the advantage of working your entire body instead of just your legs as most forms of aerobic training do.

Sample Circuit Training Workout

Begin by doing one minute of each activity and then repeating the circuit up to three times if you can. As you get stronger, you can work up to doing each activity for more minutes.

1. Jog

2. Jumping jacks

3. Jog

4. Crunches

5. Jog

6. Push-ups

7. Sprint

8. Walk

9. Knee-ups (Stand in place, bring one knee at a time up to your chest, and return to the ground.)

10. Jog

11. Jump-ups (Start by touching your toes, and then jump up as high as you can landing in a standing position; bend down, touch toes, and do again.)

12. Jog

13. Sprint

14. Walk

15. Leg raises (Lie on the ground, and put your hands under the small of your back for support. Raise both legs up about one foot off the ground, squeeze the abs, and hold for twenty seconds.)

16. Jog

17. Walking lunges

18. Jog

19. Squats (Stand with feet shoulder-width apart. Keep heels on the ground and squat down as low as you can, keeping heels on the ground.)

20. Walk

21. Sprint

22. Walk

References and Scientific Basis

This section provides sources of supportive data and explanation of the major scientific points of *Crack the Fat-Loss Code* and *Conquer the Fat-Loss Code*.

Seventy-Two-Hour Reserve Function

All supportive data is the same time-tested data already used in the "gold standard" diet books, which include the Atkins, South Beach, and Body for Life diets. This scientific point is based on carbohydrate depletion and the biochemistry of glycogen. In short, it takes three days (seventy-two hours) in an average mildly active individual to deplete the skeletal muscle of carbohydrates (glycogen). This section offers a brief explanation of glycogen biochemistry and a partial listing of relevant studies. Literally hundreds of studies have been used, for purposes of marathon runners, extreme sport racers, and bodybuilders. Dieters benefit from these studies for fat loss as well.

Biochemistry of Glycogen

Glycogen is found principally in muscle and liver cells, where it serves as a readily accessible depot for the storage of glucose. Glycogen is broken down when adenosine triphosphate (ATP) transfers intracellular energy needed by muscle cells or when blood glucose levels drop too low over a seventy-two-hour period. Glycogen is composed of linked D-glucose residues. The linkages between glucose residues are of two types: α-1,4 and α-1,6, shown in Figure 1. The importance of glycogen to our plan is in the understanding of the importance of how glycogen converts to energy. The energy is what we manipulate to ultimately satisfy the body's needs of replenishing glycogen and using fat as a source of energy, thus the creation of macro-patterning.

FIGURE 1   Glucose Linkage Residue

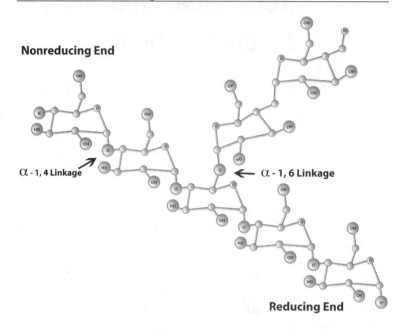

Nonreducing End

α - 1, 4 Linkage

← α - 1, 6 Linkage

Reducing End

Sources

Alonso M. D., J. Lomako, W. M. Lomako, and W. J. Whelan. 1995. "A New Look at the Biogenesis of Glycogen." *Federation of American Societies for Experimental Biology Journal* 9(12): 1126–37.

Baba, N. H., S. Sawaya, N. Torbay, A. Habbal, S. Azar, and S. A. Hashim. 1999. "High Protein vs. High Carbohydrate Hypoenergetic Diet for the Treatment of Obese Hyperinsulinemic Subjects." *International Journal of Obesity and Related Metabolic Disorders* 23(11): 1202–6.

Bergström, J., L. Hermansen, E. Hultman, and B. Saltin. 1967. "Diet, Muscle Glycogen and Physical Performance." *Acta Physiologica Scandinavica* 71(2): 140–50.

Biolo, G., R. Y. Declan Fleming, and R. R. Wolfe. 1995. "Physiologic Hyperinsulinemia Stimulates Protein Synthesis and Enhances Transport of Selected Amino Acids in Human Skeletal Muscle." *Journal of Clinical Investigation* 95(2): 811–19.

Burke, L. M., G. R. Collier, and M. Hargreaves. 1993. "Muscle Glycogen Storage After Prolonged Exercise: Effect of the Glycemic Index of Carbohydrate Feedings." *Journal of Applied Physiology* 75(2): 1019–23.

Costill, D. L., W. M. Sherman, and W. J. Fink. 1981. "The Role of Dietary Carbohydrate in Muscle Glycogen Resynthesis after Strenuous Running." *American Journal of Clinical Nutrition* 34: 1831–36.

Coyle, E. F. 1991. "Timing and Method of Increased Carbohydrate Intake to Cope with Heavy Training, Competition and Recovery." *Journal of Sports Science and Medicine* 9 (suppl): 29–52.

Danforth W. H. 1965. "Glycogen Synthetase Activity in Skeletal Muscle: Interconversion of Two Forms and Control of Glycogen Synthesis." *Journal of Biological Chemistry* 240 (February): 588–93.

Hers, H. G., and L. Hue. 1983. Gluconeogenesis and Related Aspects of Glycolysis." *Annual Review of Biochemistry* 52: 617–53.

Ivy, J. L., M. C. Lee, and M. J. Reed. 1988. "Muscle Glycogen Storage After Different Amounts of Carbohydrate Ingestion." *Journal of Applied Physiology* 65: 20,018–23.

Kirsch, K. A., and H. von Ameln. 1981. "Feeding Patterns of Endurance Athletes." *European Journal of Applied Physiology* 47: 197–208.

Roberts, K. M., E. G. Noble, D. B. Hayden, and A. W. Taylor. 1988. "Simple and Complex Carbohydrate-Rich Diets and Muscle Glycogen Content of Marathon Runners." *European Journal of Applied Physiology* 57: 70–74.

Forty-Eight-Hour Conserve Function

The body's conservation of energy expenditure is well supported by many medical and scientific studies done on how restrictive food intake or harsh dieting affects the metabolic rate. Energy expenditure encompasses many factors, including resting metabolic rate (RMR), thermic effect of food (TEF), thermic effect of activity (TEA), and thermic effect of stress (TES). All these factors play a role in the total energy expenditure. Along with the following partial list of relevant studies, there are hundreds of studies that date from 1969 to the present day.

Sources

Abbott, W., et al. 1990. "Energy Expenditure in Humans: Effects of Dietary Fat and Carbohydrate." *American Journal of Physiology* 258 (2 pt. 1): E347–51.

Booth, Frank, Ph.D. "University of Missouri at Columbia Study Concluded That the Fat Cells in Lab Rats Can Increase in Size by 25% After 48 Hours of Missed Exercise." *Women's Health*, March 2007.

Borel, M., et al. 1984. "Estimation of Energy Expenditure and Maintenance Energy Requirements of College-Age Men and Women." *American Journal of Clinical Nutrition* 40(6): 1264–72.

Bray, G. 1969. "Effect of Caloric Intake on Energy Expenditure in Obese Subjects." *Lancet* 2: 397–98.

Brillon, D., et al. 1995. "Effect of Cortisol on Energy Expenditure and Amino Acid Metabolism in Humans." *American Journal of Physiology* 268: E501–13.

Bullough, C. R., C. A. Gilette, M. A. Harris, and C. L. Melby. 1995. "Interaction of Acute Changes in Exercise Energy Expenditure and Energy Intake on Resting Metabolic Rate." *American Journal of Clinical Nutrition* 61: 473–81.

deGroot, L., et al. 1989. "Adaptation of Energy Metabolism of Overweight Women to Alternating and Continuous Low Energy Intake." *American Journal of Clinical Nutrition* 50(6): 1314–23.

Foster, G., et al. 1990. "Controlled Trial of the Metabolic Effects of a Very-Low-Calorie Diet: Short- and Long-Term Effects." *American Journal of Clinical Nutrition* 51(2): 167–72.

Garby, L., et al. 1988. "Effect of 12 Weeks' Light-Moderate Underfeeding on 24-Hour Energy Expenditure in Normal Male and Female Subjects." *European Journal of Clinical Nutrition* 42(4): 295–300.

Henson, L., et al. 1987. "Effects of Exercise Training on Resting Energy Expenditure During Caloric Restriction." *American Journal of Clinical Nutrition* 46(6): 893–99.

Lee, R., and D. Nieman. 2003. *Nutritional Assessment*, 3rd ed. Boston: McGraw-Hill, 233.

Luscombe, N., et al. 2002. "Effects of Energy-Restricted Diets Containing Increased Protein on Weight Loss, Resting Energy Expenditure and Thermic Effect of Feeding in Type II Diabetes." *Diabetes Care* 25(4): 652–57.

Molé, P. A., J. S. Stern, C. L. Schultz, E. M. Bernauer, and B. J. Holcom. 1989. "Exercise Reverses Depressed Metabolic Rate Produced by Severe Caloric Restriction." *Medicine and Science in Sports and Exercise* 21(1): 29–33.

Mulligan, K., and G. E. Butterfield. 1990. "Discrepancies Between Energy Intake and Expenditure in Physically Active Women." *British Journal of Nutrition* 64: 23–36.

Utter, A. C., D. C. Nieman, E. M. Shannonhouse, D. E. Butterworth, and C. N. Nieman. 1998. "Influence of Diet and/or Exercise on Body Composition and Cardiorespiratory Fitness in Obese Women." *International Journal of Sport Nutrition* 8(3): 213–22.

Velthuis-te Weirik, E., et al. 1995. "Impact of a Moderately Energy Restricted Diet on Energy Metabolism and Body Composition in Non-Obese Men." *International Journal of Obesity and Related Metabolic Disorders* 19(5): 318–24.

Adaptive Response—Dieter's Plateau

The regulating by the body of its intake and expenditure is the major key to understanding the set-point theory of body weight. It is said that the hypothalamus and autonomic nervous system achieve something known by the body as homeostasis, or maintaining the body's status quo. Factors such as blood pressure, body temperature, fluid and electrolyte balance, and body weight are held to a precise value called the set point. Although this set point can migrate over time, from day to day it is remarkably fixed. To be successful over the long term, any diet must overcome the body's response to adapt. The set-point theory is a very old scientific study that has resurfaced recently and has made its way into many recent diet books. The following articles are just a small selection of the cited research on the set-point theory.

Sources

Chant, W. L. 2003. "The Body's Adaptive Ability Explained." Altamonte Springs, FL: *ForeverFit Nutrition Boot Camp Advanced Manual.*

Harris, R. B. 1990. "Role of Set-Point Theory in Regulation of Body Weight." *Federation of American Societies for Experimental Biology Journal* 4: 3310–18.

Keesey, R. E., and M. D. Hirvonen. 1997. "Body Weight Set-Points: Determination and Adjustment." *Journal of Nutrition* 127 (suppl.): 1875S–83S.

Index

About the Author and ForeverFit®

About Wendy Chant

Wendy Chant is the author of the *New York Times* bestselling *Crack the Fat-Loss Code*. She is a certified master personal trainer (MPT) and specialist in performance nutrition (SPN), with a bachelor of science degree in medical sciences and nutrition science.

Beginning her career as a personal trainer with Bally Total Fitness, Wendy quickly achieved a national ranking as one of the top ten in personal training. Her commitment to helping others achieve their goals inspired the opening of her own training studio, ForeverFit, in 1998.

As a specialist in performance nutrition, Wendy was one of the first in her field to truly embrace the philosophy of food coaching, which is tailored to clients' particular goals, with the aim of making them feel fantastic on all levels: health, vitality, moods, and weight, as well as gaining confidence in their food choices and body image. She has become a nationally sought-after food coach.

A former marathon runner and champion bodybuilder who competed on the national level, Wendy has since focused all of her attention on spreading the ForeverFit message. From her corporate offices in Central Florida, she divides her busy schedule among running her individual Nutrition Boot Camp™ classes, nurturing a full speaking schedule, and holding seminars and workshops.

About ForeverFit

ForeverFit programs and services are offered at Wendy's national headquarters in Central Florida and can be found online at join foreverfit.com.

Long before writing *Crack the Fat-Loss Code* and *Conquer the Fat-Loss Code*, she taught classes and coached clients on the 72/48 code, macro-patterning, and meal planning. If you're interested in more information on these programs, look through the following categories and see which best fits your needs. No matter where you live, the program has you covered with three ways to benefit from this intensive hands-on instruction. So when you're ready, simply click, write, or call, and Wendy and her team at ForeverFit will be glad to personally help you take fat loss to a whole new level.

• **Conquer the Fat-Loss Code with Nutrition Boot Camp DVD:** For your convenience, the entire eight-week program using the *Crack the Fat Loss Code* and *Conquer the Fat-Loss Code* philosophy is available on a one-of-a-kind DVD uniquely designed to walk you through the program week by week. Through this entertaining and informative DVD, you can educate yourself on all the vital information about your body and how it responds to food. You will also hear the stories of countless boot camp "code crackers" who have changed their lives forever using this revolutionary program. The DVD comes with a companion guide that has the entire eight-week daily menu and an easy substitutions list. Visit joinforeverfit.com to watch a preview and to see and hear success stories from many code crackers using Wendy's program.

• **Eight-week classes in Central Florida and national weekend boot camps:** Wendy's program began as an informative class format for people seeking the truth about fat loss and dieting. Since then, these one-of-a-kind programs have been attended by thousands, and Wendy, today's fitness authority, not only guides her students to fat-loss success but also gives information and advice on exercise, supplementation, and how to achieve a better body. Remember her motto: "Better health and better life." This class is available for anyone in the country via video-on-demand. You can actually be one of the many people taking this class over the Internet from your own home.

• **Exclusive food coaching with Wendy Chant—in person, online, via webcam, and by phone and fax:** Couldn't everyone use a food coach? Well, you can't go wrong when Wendy personally guides you through the *Conquer the Fat-Loss Code* process. She takes a personal interest in all of her students' successes. Whether you're right in front of her or thousands of miles away, you will never have guilt or worries about food when Wendy is your coach. You can now access her via live video through Skype; all you need is a webcam. You can download Skype free and then sign up through the online store to be coached by Wendy.

• **Website resources and member area:** The ForeverFit website is chock-full of resources, with such features as an events calendar, forums, and a section where you can ask questions, look for advice, or share your stories with others. The site also offers many video-on-demand and pay-per-view programs so you can download exercise programs and more delicious recipes. Also look for Wendy's future Internet and radio talk shows.

• **ForeverFit supplement line:** Wendy has personally developed a line of supplements that is available through her online store. Also available are top-quality protein powders suggested by Wendy, including her own brand, Wendy's Whey—a protein with no preservatives or artificial sweeteners.

• **Toll-free number:** You can always reach ForeverFit on the toll-free number at (866) 865-9110 or through the website at www.joinforeverfit.com. Or if you're visiting Florida, why not stop by the corporate offices in Altamonte Springs?

One scientific approach to weight loss that finally cracks the code.

How do you lose weight without hitting the dreaded plateau?

Using a proven combination of food, exercise, and "macropatterning," expert Wendy Chant figured out how to "trick" the body into losing weight. This is one breakthrough plan that actually works.

THE NEW YORK TIMES BESTSELLER!

CRACK THE FAT-LOSS CODE

LOSE UP TO 25 POUNDS IN 8 WEEKS AND KEEP IT OFF

Outsmart Your Metabolism and Conquer the Diet Plateau

WENDY CHANT, MPT, SPN
FOUNDER OF FOREVERFIT®
FOREWORD BY SERGIO ZAMORA, M.D., FACS